W9-DDA-306

A TRACT ON
MONETARY REFORM

A TRACT ON
MONETARY REFORM

John Maynard Keynes

GREAT MINDS SERIES

Prometheus Books

59 John Glenn Drive
Amherst, New York 14228-2197

SCCCC - LIBRARY
St. Peters, MO
WITHDRAWN

Published 2000 by
Prometheus Books
59 John Glenn Drive
Amherst, New York 14228–2197
VOICE: 716–691–0133, ext. 207
FAX: 716–691–0137
WWW.PROMETHEUSBOOKS.COM

Library of Congress Cataloging-in-Publication Data

Keynes, John Maynard, 1883–1946.
    A tract on monetary reform / John Maynard Keynes.
        p. cm. — (Great minds series)
    Originally published: London : Macmillan, 1924.
    Includes bibliographical references and index.
    ISBN 1–57392–793–7 (pbk. : alk. paper)
    1. Monetary policy. 2. Keynesian economics. I. Title.
II. Series.

HG221 .K4 1999
332.4'6—dc21
                                            99–057749
                                               CIP

Printed in the United States of America on acid-free paper.

Great Minds Paperback Series

Nicolaus Copernicus,
On the Revolutions of Heavenly Spheres

Charles Darwin, *The Descent of Man*

Charles Darwin, *The Origin of Species*

Charles Darwin, *The Voyage of the* Beagle

Emile Durkheim,
Ethics and the Sociology of Morals

Albert Einstein, *Relativity*

Desiderius Erasmus, *The Praise of Folly*

Michael Faraday, *The Forces of Matter*

Sigmund Freud, *Totem and Taboo*

Galileo Galilei,
Dialogues Concerning Two New Sciences

Edward Gibbon, *On Christianity*

Charlotte Perkins Gilman,
Women and Economics

Ernst Haeckel, *The Riddle of the Universe*

Alexander Hamilton, John Jay,
and James Madison, *The Federalist*

William Harvey,
*On the Motion of the Heart and Blood
in Animals*

Werner Heisenberg,
Physics and Philosophy

Herodotus, *The History*

Julian Huxley, *Evolutionary Humanism*

Thomas Henry Huxley,
*Agnosticism and Christianity
and Other Essays*

Edward Jenner,
Vaccination against Smallpox

Johannes Kepler,
Epitome of Copernican Astronomy
and *Harmonies of the World*

John Maynard Keynes,
*The General Theory of Employment,
Interest, and Money*

John Maynard Keynes,
A Tract on Monetary Reform

Thomas R. Malthus,
An Essay on the Principle of Population

Alfred Marshall, *Principles of Economics*

Karl Marx, *Theories of Surplus Value*

Isaac Newton, *The Principia*

Louis Pasteur and Joseph Lister,
*Germ Theory and Its Application to
Medicine* and *On the Antiseptic Principle
of the Practice of Surgery*

Ernest Renan, *The Life of Jesus*

David Ricardo, *Principles of Political
Economy and Taxation*

Adam Smith, *The Wealth of Nations*

Elizabeth Cady Stanton,
The Woman's Bible

Jonathan Swift,
A Modest Proposal and Other Satires

Thucydides,
History of the Peloponnesian War

Thorstein Veblen,
The Theory of the Leisure Class

Voltaire, *A Treatise on Toleration
and Other Essays*

Alfred Russel Wallace, *Island Life*

H. G. Wells, *The Conquest of Time*

Andrew D. White,
*A History of the Warfare of Science
with Theology in Christendom*

See the back of this volume for a complete list of titles in Prometheus's
Great Books in Philosophy and Great Minds series.

JOHN MAYNARD KEYNES was born in Cambridge, England, on July 5,1883. His father, John Neville Keynes, was a professor and administrator at Cambridge University, and himself the author of *The Scope and Methods of Political Economy*.

After attending Eton (1897–1902), Keynes entered King's College, where he studied economics. Following graduation, he worked in the India Office (1906–1908); lectured on economics at Cambridge (1908); was made a fellow of King's College (1909), editor of the *Economic Journal,* and secretary of the Royal Economic Society (1911); and accepted a position in the British treasury.

In 1919 Keynes was principal representative of the treasury at the Paris Peace Conference. Disturbed by developments at the conference, however, he soon resigned. His *Economic Consequences of the Peace* (1919) gave voice to his strong objection to the punitive measures being enacted against Germany. In this eloquently argued and strangely prescient work, Keynes detailed the problems that would result from the war reparations to be made by conquered Germany beyond her ability to pay, as well as the devastating economic, social, and political consequences of continuing European ultranationalism.

Keynes returned to England to resume teaching at Cambridge (1920–1937). It was at this time that he wrote his main work, *The General Theory of Employment, Interest, and Money* (1936). Critiquing the neoclassical theory of Alfred Marshall, namely, that a normally functioning market economy leads to full employment, Keynes showed that a market economy can operate at less than full employment, and that it may even work against reducing unemployment. Keynes advocated enlightened government intervention over unregulated laissez-faire policies. The Keynesian analysis of how monetary and financial arrangements affect the economy has formed the basis of subsequent activist governmental fiscal and monetary policy.

Heart trouble ended Keynes's academic career in 1937. However, he remained active as an adviser to the chancellor of the exchequer (1940), and as principal British delegate and negotiator at the Bretton Woods Conference (1944), Stage II of Lend Lease (1944), arrangements for a United States loan to Britain (1945), and the inauguration of the International Monetary Fund and the International Bank (1946). In 1942, he was raised to the peerage, being named 1st Baron Keynes of Tilton. John Maynard Keynes died in Firle, Sussex, on April 21, 1946.

Keynes's other published works include *A Revision of the Treaty* (1922), *A Tract on Monetary Reform* (1923), *A Treatise on Money* (1930), and *How to Pay for the War* (1940).

PREFACE

WE leave Saving to the private investor, and we encourage him to place his savings mainly in titles to money. We leave the responsibility for setting Production in motion to the business man, who is mainly influenced by the profits which he expects to accrue to himself in terms of money. Those who are not in favour of drastic changes in the existing organisation of society believe that these arrangements, being in accord with human nature, have great advantages. But they cannot work properly if the money, which they assume as a stable measuring-rod, is undependable. Unemployment, the precarious life of the worker, the disappointment of expectation, the sudden loss of savings, the excessive windfalls to individuals, the speculator, the profiteer—all proceed, in large measure, from the instability of the standard of value.

It is often supposed that the costs of production are threefold, corresponding to the rewards of labour, enterprise, and accumulation. But there is a fourth cost, namely risk ; and the reward of risk-bearing is one of the heaviest, and perhaps the most avoidable, burden on production. This element of risk is greatly aggravated by the instability of the standard of value. Currency Reforms, which led to the adoption by this country and the world at large of sound monetary principles, would diminish the wastes of *Risk*, which consume at present too much of our estate.

Nowhere do conservative notions consider themselves more in place than in currency ; yet nowhere is the need of innovation more urgent. One is often warned that a scientific treatment of currency questions is impossible because the banking world is intellectually incapable of understanding its own problems. If this is true, the order of Society, which they stand for, will decay. But I do not believe it. What we have lacked is a clear analysis of the real facts, rather than ability to understand an analysis already given. If the new ideas, now developing in many quarters, are sound and right, I do not doubt that sooner or later they will prevail. I dedicate this book, humbly and without permission, to the Governors and Court of the Bank of England, who now and for the future have a much more difficult and anxious task entrusted to them than in former days.

J. M. KEYNES.

October 1923.

CONTENTS

CHAPTER IV

CHAPTER V

[I have utilised, mainly in the first chapter and in parts of the second and third, the material, much revised and re-written, of some articles which were published during 1922 in the Reconstruction Supplements of the *Manchester Guardian Commercial.*— J. M. K.]

CHAPTER I

THE CONSEQUENCES TO SOCIETY OF CHANGES IN THE VALUE OF MONEY

MONEY is only important for what it will procure. Thus a change in the monetary unit, which is uniform in its operation and affects all transactions equally, has no consequences. If, by a change in the established standard of value, a man received and owned twice as much money as he did before in payment for all rights and for all efforts, and if he also paid out twice as much money for all acquisitions and for all satisfactions, he would be wholly unaffected.

It follows, therefore, that a change in the value of money, that is to say in the level of prices, is important to Society only in so far as its incidence is unequal. Such changes have produced in the past, and are producing now, the vastest social consequences, because, as we all know, when the value of money changes, it does *not* change equally for all persons or for all purposes. A man's receipts and his outgoings are not all modified in one uniform proportion. Thus a change in prices and rewards, as measured in money, generally affects different classes unequally, transfers wealth from one to another, bestows affluence here and embarrassment there, and redistributes Fortune's favours so as to frustrate design and disappoint expectation.

The fluctuations in the value of money since 1914 have been on a scale so great as to constitute, with all that they involve, one of the most significant events in the economic history of the modern world. The fluctuation of the standard, whether gold, silver, or paper, has not only been of unprecedented violence, but has been visited on a society of which the economic organisation is more dependent than that of any earlier epoch on the assumption that the standard of value would be moderately stable.

During the Napoleonic Wars and the period immediately succeeding them the extreme fluctuation of English prices within a single year was 22 per cent; and the highest price level reached during the first quarter of the nineteenth century, which we used to reckon the most disturbed period of our currency history, was less than double the lowest and with an interval of thirteen years. Compare with this the extraordinary movements of the past nine years. To recall the reader's mind to the exact facts, I refer him to the table on the next page.

I have not included those countries—Russia, Poland, and Austria—where the old currency has long been bankrupt. But it will be observed that, even apart from the countries which have suffered revolution or defeat, no quarter of the world has escaped a violent movement. In the United States, where the gold standard has functioned unabated, in Japan, where the war brought with it more profit than liability, in the neutral country of Sweden, the changes in the value of money have been comparable with those in the United Kingdom.

INDEX NUMBERS OF WHOLESALE PRICES EXPRESSED AS A PERCENTAGE OF 1913 (1).

Monthly Average.	United Kingdom (2).	France.	Italy.	Germany.	U.S.A. (3).	Canada.	Japan.	Sweden.	India.
1913	100	100	100	100	100	100	100	100	..
1914	100	102	96	106	98	100	95	116	100
1915	127	140	133	142	101	109	97	145	112
1916	160	189	201	153	127	134	117	185	128
1917	206	262	299	179	177	175	149	244	147
1918	227	340	409	217	194	205	196	339	180
1919	242	357	364	415	206	216	239	330	198
1920	295	510	624	1,486	226	250	260	347	204
1921	182	345	577	1,911	147	182	200	211	181
1922	159	327	562	34,182	149	165	196	162	180
1923*	159	411	582	765,000	157	167	192	166	179

(1) These figures are taken from the *Monthly Bulletin of Statistics* of the League of Nations. (2) *Statist* up to 1919; thereafter the median of the *Economist, Statist*, and Board of Trade Index Numbers. (3) Bureau of Labour Index Number (revised).

* First half-year.

From 1914 to 1920 all these countries experienced an expansion in the supply of money to spend relatively to the supply of things to purchase, that is to say *Inflation*. Since 1920 those countries which have regained control of their financial situation, not content with bringing the Inflation to an end, have contracted their supply of money and have experienced the fruits of *Deflation*. Others have followed inflationary courses more riotously than before. In a few, of which Italy is one, an imprudent desire to deflate has been balanced by the intractability of the financial situation, with the happy result of comparatively stable prices.

Each process, Inflation and Deflation alike, has inflicted great injuries. Each has an effect in altering the *distribution* of wealth between different classes, Inflation in this respect being the worse of the two. Each has also an effect in overstimulating or retarding the *production* of wealth, though here Deflation is the more injurious. The division of our subject thus indicated is the most convenient for us to follow,— examining first the effect of changes in the value of money on the distribution of wealth with most of our attention on Inflation, and next their effect on the production of wealth with most of our attention on Deflation. How have the price changes of the past nine years affected the productivity of the community as a whole, and how have they affected the conflicting interests and mutual relations of its component classes ? The answer to these questions will serve to establish the gravity of the evils, into the remedy for which it is the object of this book to inquire.

I.—Changes in the Value of Money, as affecting Distribution

For the purpose of this inquiry a triple classification of Society is convenient—into the Investing Class, the Business Class, and the Earning Class. These classes overlap, and the same individual may earn, deal, and invest; but in the present organisation of society such a division corresponds to a social cleavage and an actual divergence of interest.

1. *The Investing Class.*

Of the various purposes which money serves, some essentially depend upon the assumption that its real value is nearly constant over a period of time. The chief of these are those connected, in a wide sense, with contracts for the *investment of money*. Such contracts—namely, those which provide for the payment of fixed sums of money over a long period of time—are the characteristic of what it is convenient to call the *Investment System*, as distinct from the property system generally.

Under this phase of capitalism, as developed during the nineteenth century, many arrangements were devised for separating the management of property from its ownership. These arrangements were of three leading types: (1) Those in which the proprietor, while parting with the management of his property, retained his ownership of it—*i.e.* of the actual land, buildings, and machinery, or of whatever else it consisted in, this mode of tenure being typified by a holding of ordinary shares in a joint-stock company ; (2) those in which he parted with the property temporarily, receiving a fixed sum of *money* annually in the meantime, but regained his property eventually, as typified by a lease ; and (3) those in which he parted with his real property permanently, in return either for a perpetual annuity fixed in terms of money, or for a terminable annuity and the repayment of the principal in money at the end of the term, as typified by mortgages, bonds, debentures, and preference shares. This third type represents the full development of *Investment*.

Contracts to receive fixed sums of money at future dates (made without provision for possible changes in the real value of money at those dates) must have existed as long as money has been lent and borrowed. In the form of leases and mortgages, and also of permanent loans to Governments and to a few private bodies, such as the East India Company, they were already frequent in the eighteenth century. But during the nineteenth century they developed a new and increased importance, and had, by the beginning of the twentieth, divided the propertied classes into two groups—the " business men " and the " investors "—with partly divergent interests. The division was not sharp as between individuals; for business men might be investors also, and investors might hold ordinary shares; but the division was nevertheless real, and not the less important because it was seldom noticed.

By this system the active business class could call to the aid of their enterprises not only their own wealth but the savings of the whole community; and the professional and propertied classes, on the other hand, could find an employment for their resources, which involved them in little trouble, no responsibility, and (it was believed) small risk.

For a hundred years the system worked, throughout Europe, with an extraordinary success and facilitated the growth of wealth on an unprecedented scale. To save and to invest became at once the duty and the delight of a large class. The savings were seldom drawn on, and, accumulating at compound interest, made possible the material triumphs which we now all take for granted. The morals, the politics, the literature, and the religion of the age joined in a grand conspiracy for the promotion of saving. God and Mammon were reconciled. Peace on earth to men of good means. A rich man could, after all, enter into the Kingdom of Heaven—if only he saved. A new harmony sounded from the celestial spheres. " It is curious to observe how, through the wise and beneficent arrangement of Providence, men thus do the greatest service to the public, when they are thinking of nothing but their own gain " [1] ; so sang the angels.

The atmosphere thus created well harmonised the demands of expanding business and the needs of an expanding population with the growth of a comfortable non-business class. But amidst the general enjoyment of ease and progress, the extent, to which the system depended on the stability of the money to which the investing classes had committed their fortunes, was generally overlooked ; and an unquestioning confidence was apparently felt that this matter would look after itself. Investments spread and multiplied, until, for the middle classes of the world, the gilt-edged bond came to typify all that was most permanent and most secure. So rooted in our day has been the conventional belief in the stability and safety of a money contract that, according to English law, trustees have been encouraged to embark their trust funds exclusively in such transactions, and are indeed forbidden, except in the case of real estate (an exception which is itself a survival of the conditions of an earlier age), to employ them otherwise.[2]

As in other respects, so also in this, the nineteenth century relied on the future permanence of its own

---

[1] *Easy Lessons on Money Matters for the Use of Young People.* Published by the Society for Promoting Christian Knowledge. Twelfth Edition, 1850.

[2] German trustees were not released from a similar obligation until 1923, by which date the value of trust funds invested in titles to money had entirely disappeared.

happy experiences and disregarded the warning of past misfortunes. It chose to forget that there is no historical warrant for expecting money to be represented even by a constant quantity of a particular metal, far less by a constant purchasing power. Yet Money is simply that which the State declares from time to time to be a good legal discharge of money contracts. In 1914 gold had not been the English standard for a century or the sole standard of any other country for half a century. There is no record of a prolonged war or a great social upheaval which has not been accompanied by a change in the legal tender, but an almost unbroken chronicle in every country which has a history, back to the earliest dawn of economic record, of a progressive deterioration in the real value of the successive legal tenders which have represented money.

Moreover, this progressive deterioration in the value of money through history is not an accident, and has had behind it two great driving forces— the impecuniosity of Governments and the superior political influence of the debtor class.

The power of taxation by currency depreciation is one which has been inherent in the State since Rome discovered it. The creation of legal-tender has been and is a Government's ultimate reserve ; and no State or Government is likely to decree its own bankruptcy or its own downfall, so long as this instrument still lies at hand unused.

Besides this, as we shall see below, the benefits of a depreciating currency are not restricted to the Government. Farmers and debtors and all persons liable to pay fixed money dues share in the advantage. As now in the persons of business men, so also in former ages these classes constituted the active and constructive elements in the economic scheme. Those secular changes, therefore, which in the past have depreciated money, assisted the new men and emancipated them from the dead hand; they benefited new wealth at the expense of old, and armed enterprise against accumulation. The tendency of money to depreciate has been in past times a weighty counterpoise against the cumulative results of compound interest and the inheritance of fortunes. It has been a loosening influence against the rigid distribution of old-won wealth and the separation of ownership from activity. By this means each generation can disinherit in part its predecessors' heirs; and the project of founding a perpetual fortune must be disappointed in this way, unless the community with conscious deliberation provides against it in some other way, more equitable and more expedient.

At any rate, under the influence of these two forces—the financial necessities of Governments and the political influence of the debtor class—sometimes the one and sometimes the other, the progress of inflation has been *continuous*, if we consider long periods, ever since money was first devised in the sixth century B.C. Sometimes the standard of value has depreciated of itself; failing this, debasements have done the work.

Nevertheless it is easy at all times, as a result of the way we use money in daily life, to forget all this and to look on money as itself the absolute standard of value; and when, besides, the actual events of a hundred years have not disturbed his illusions, the average man regards what has been normal for three generations as a part of the permanent social fabric.

The course of events during the nineteenth century favoured such ideas. During its first quarter, the very high prices of the Napoleonic Wars were followed by a somewhat rapid improvement in the value of money. For the next seventy years, with some temporary fluctuations, the tendency of prices continued to be downwards, the lowest point being reached in 1896. But while this was the tendency as regards direction, the remarkable feature of this long period was the relative *stability* of the price level. Approximately the *same* level of price ruled in or about the years 1826, 1841, 1855, 1862, 1867, 1871, and 1915. Prices were also level in the years 1844, 1881, and 1914. If we call the index number of these latter years 100, we find that, for the period of close on a century from 1826 to the outbreak of war, the maximum fluctuation in either direction was

30 points, the index number never rising above 130
and never falling below 70.   No wonder that we came
to believe in the stability of money contracts over
a long period.   The metal *gold* might not possess
all the theoretical advantages of an artificially regulated standard, but it could not be tampered with and
had proved reliable in practice.

At the same time, the investor in Consols in the
early part of the century had done very well in three
different ways.   The " security " of his investment
had come to be considered as near absolute perfection
as was possible.   Its capital value had uniformly
appreciated, partly for the reason just stated, but
chiefly because the steady fall in the rate of interest
increased the number of years' purchase of the annual
income which represented the capital.[1]   And the
annual money income had a purchasing power which
on the whole was increasing.   If, for example, we
consider the seventy years from 1826 to 1896 (and
ignore the great improvement immediately after
Waterloo), we find that the capital value of Consols
rose steadily, with only temporary set-backs, from
79 to 109 (in spite of Goschen's conversion from
a 3 per cent rate to a $2\frac{3}{4}$ per cent rate in 1889 and
a $2\frac{1}{2}$ per cent rate effective in 1903), while the purchasing power of the annual dividends, even after allowing
for the reduced rates of interest, had increased 50 per

---

[1] If (for example) the rate of interest falls from $4\frac{1}{2}$ per cent to 3 per
cent, 3 per cent Consols rise in value from 66 to 100.

cent. But Consols, too, had added the virtue of stability to that of improvement. Except in years of crisis Consols never fell below 90 during the reign of Queen Victoria ; and even in '48, when thrones were crumbling, the mean price of the year fell but 5 points. Ninety when she ascended the throne, they reached their maximum with her in the year of Diamond Jubilee. What wonder that our parents thought Consols a good investment !

Thus there grew up during the nineteenth century a large, powerful, and greatly respected class of persons, well-to-do individually and very wealthy in the aggregate, who owned neither buildings, nor land, nor businesses, nor precious metals, but titles to an annual income in legal-tender money. In particular, that peculiar creation and pride of the nineteenth century, the savings of the middle class, had been mainly thus embarked. Custom and favourable experience had acquired for such investments an unimpeachable reputation for security.

Before the war these medium fortunes had already begun to suffer some loss (as compared with the summit of their prosperity in the middle 'nineties) from the rise in prices and also in the rate of interest. But the monetary events which have accompanied and have followed the war have taken from them about one-half of their real value in England, seven-eighths in France, eleven-twelfths in Italy, and virtually the whole in Germany and in the succession states of Austria - Hungary and Russia.

The loss to the typical English investor of the pre-war period is sufficiently measured by the loss to the investor in Consols. Such an investor, as we have already seen, was steadily improving his position, apart from temporary fluctuations, up to 1896, and in this and the following year two maxima were reached simultaneously — both the capital value of an annuity and also the purchasing power of money. Between 1896 and 1914, on the other hand, the investor had already suffered a serious loss—the capital value of his annuity had fallen by about a third, and the purchasing power of his income had also fallen by nearly a third. This loss, however, was incurred gradually over a period of nearly twenty years from an exceptional maximum, and did not leave him appreciably worse off than he had been in the early 'eighties or the early 'forties. But upon the top of this came the further swifter loss of the war period. Between 1914 and 1920 the capital value of the investor's annuity again fell by more than a third, and the purchasing power of his income by about two-thirds. In addition, the standard rate of income tax rose from $7\frac{1}{2}$ per cent in 1914 to 30 per cent in 1921.[1] Roughly estimated in round numbers, the change may be represented thus in

---

[1] Since 1896 there has been the further burden of the Death Duties.

terms of an index of which the base year is
1914:

	Purchasing Power of the Income of Consols.[1]	Do. after deduction of Income Tax at the standard rate.	Money price of the capital value of Consols.	Purchasing Power of the capital value of Consols.
1815	61	59	92	56
1826	85	90	108	92
1841	85	90	122	104
1869	87	89	127	111
1883	104	108	138	144
1896	139	145	150	208
1914	100	100	100	100
1920	34	26	64	22
1921	53	39	56	34
1922	62	50	76	47

The second column well illustrates what a splendid
investment gilt - edged stocks had been through
the century from Waterloo to Mons, even if we omit
altogether the abnormal values of 1896–97. Our
table shows how the epoch of Diamond Jubilee was
the culminating moment in the prosperity of the
British middle class. But it also exhibits with the
precision of figures the familiar bewailed plight of
those who try to live on the income of the same
trustee investments as before the war. The owner
of consols in 1922 had a real income, one half of
what he had in 1914 and one third of what he had
in 1896. The whole of the improvement of the
nineteenth century had been obliterated, and his

[1] Without allowance for the reduction of the interest from 3 to 2½ per
cent

situation was not quite so good as it had been after Waterloo.

Some mitigating circumstances should not be overlooked. Whilst the war was a period of the dissipation of the community's resources as a whole, it was a period of saving for the individuals of the saving class, who with their larger holdings of the securities of the Government now have an increased aggregate money claim on the receipts of the Exchequer. Also, the investing class, which has lost money, overlaps, both socially and by the ties of family, with the business class, which has made money, sufficiently to break in many cases the full severity of the loss. Moreover, in England, there has been a substantial recovery from the low point of 1920.

But these things do not wash away the significance of the facts. The effect of the war, and of the monetary policy which has accompanied and followed it, has been to take away a large part of the real value of the possessions of the investing class. The loss has been so rapid and so intermixed in the time of its occurrence with other worse losses that its full measure is not yet separately apprehended. But it has effected, nevertheless, a far-reaching change in the relative position of different classes. Throughout the Continent the pre-war savings of the middle class, so far as they were invested in bonds, mortgages, or bank deposits, have been largely or entirely wiped out. Nor can it be doubted that this experience must modify social psychology towards the practice of saving and investment. What was deemed most secure has proved least so. He who neither spent nor " speculated," who made " proper provision for his family," who sang hymns to security and observed most straitly the morals of the edified and the respectable injunctions of the worldly-wise,—he, indeed, who gave fewest pledges to Fortune has yet suffered her heaviest visitations.

What moral for our present purpose should we draw from this ? Chiefly, I think, that it is not safe or fair to combine the social organisation developed during the nineteenth century (and still retained) with a *laisser-faire* policy towards the value of money. It is not true that our former arrangements have worked well. If we are to continue to draw the voluntary savings of the community into " investments," we must make it a prime object of deliberate State policy that the standard of value, in terms of which they are expressed, should be kept stable ; adjusting in other ways (calculated to touch all forms of wealth equally and not concentrated on the relatively helpless " investors ") the redistribution of the national wealth, if, in course of time, the laws of inheritance and the rate of accumulation have drained too great a proportion of the income of the active classes into the spending control of the inactive.

2. *The Business Class*

It has long been recognised, by the business world and by economists alike, that a period of rising prices acts as a stimulus to enterprise and is beneficial to business men.

In the first place there is the advantage which is the counterpart of the loss to the investing class which we have just examined. When the value of money falls, it is evident that those persons who have engaged to pay fixed sums of money yearly out of the profits of active business must benefit, since their fixed money outgoings will bear a smaller proportion than formerly to their money turnover. This benefit persists not only during the transitional period of change, but also, so far as old loans are concerned, when prices have settled down at their new and higher level. For example, the farmers throughout Europe, who had raised by mortgage the funds to purchase the land they farmed, now find themselves almost freed from the burden at the expense of the mortgagees.

But during the period of change, while prices are rising month by month, the business man has a further and greater source of windfall. Whether he is a merchant or a manufacturer, he will generally buy before he sells, and on at least a part of his stock he will run the risk of price changes. If, therefore, month after month his stock appreciates on his hands, he is always selling at a better price than he expected and securing a windfall profit upon which he had not calculated.   In such a period the business of trade becomes unduly easy.   Any one who can borrow money and is not exceptionally unlucky must make a profit, which he may have done little to deserve.   The continuous enjoyment of such profits engenders an expectation of their renewal.   The practice of borrowing from banks is extended beyond what is normal.   If the market expects prices to rise still further, it is natural that stocks of commodities should be held speculatively for the rise, and for a time the mere expectation of a rise is sufficient, by inducing speculative purchases, to produce one.

Minsky

Take, for example, the *Statist* index number for raw materials month by month from April, 1919, to March, 1920 :

April, 1919	.	.	. 100	October	.	.	.	. 127
May	.	.	. 108	November	.	.	. 131
June	.	.	. 112	December	.	.	. 135
July	.	.	. 117	January, 1920	.	.	. 142
August	.	.	. 120	February	.	.	. 150
September	.	.	. 121	March	.	.	. 146

It follows from this table that a man, who borrowed money from his banker and used the proceeds to purchase raw materials selected at random, stood to make a profit in every single month of this period with the exception of the last, and would have cleared 46 per cent on the average of the year.   Yet bankers were not charging at this time above 7 per cent for their advances, leaving a clear profit of between

30 and 40 per cent per annum, without the exercise
of any particular skill, to any person lucky enough
to have embarked on these courses. How much
more were the opportunities of persons whose business
position and expert knowledge enabled them to
exercise intelligent anticipation as to the probable
course of prices of particular commodities! Yet
any dealer in or user of raw materials on a large
scale who knew his trade was thus situated. The
profits of certain kinds of business to the man who
has a little skill or some luck are certain in such a
period to be inordinate. Great fortunes may be made
in a few months. But apart from all such, the steady-
going business man, who would be pained and insulted
at the thought of being designated speculator or
profiteer, may find windfall profits dropping into his
lap which he has neither sought nor desired.

Economists draw an instructive distinction between what are termed the " money " rate of interest
and the " real " rate of interest. If a sum of money
worth 100 in terms of commodities at the time when
the loan is made is lent for a year at 5 per cent interest,
and is only worth 90 in terms of commodities at the
end of the year, the lender receives back, including his
interest, what is only worth $94\frac{1}{2}$. This is expressed
by saying that while the *money* rate of interest was
5 per cent, the *real* rate of interest had actually been
negative and equal to *minus* $5\frac{1}{2}$ per cent. In the
same way, if at the end of the period the value of

money had risen and the capital sum lent had come to be worth 110 in terms of commodities, while the *money* rate of interest would still be 5 per cent the *real* rate of interest would have been $15\frac{1}{2}$ per cent.

Such considerations, even though they are not explicitly present to the minds of the business world, are far from being academic. The business world may speak, and even think, as though the money rate of interest could be considered by itself, without reference to the real rate. But it does not act so. The merchant or manufacturer, who is calculating whether a 7 per cent bank rate is so onerous as to compel him to curtail his operations, is very much influenced by his anticipations about the prospective price of the commodity in which he is interested.

Thus, when prices are rising, the business man who borrows money is able to repay the lender with what, in terms of real value, not only represents no interest, but is even less than the capital originally advanced; that is, the real rate of interest falls to a negative value, and the borrower reaps a corresponding benefit. It is true that, in so far as a rise of prices is foreseen, attempts to get advantage from this by increased borrowing force the money rates of interest to move upwards. It is for this reason, amongst others, that a high bank rate should be associated with a period of rising prices, and a low bank rate with a period of falling prices. The apparent abnormality of the money rate of interest at such times is merely the other side of the attempt of the real rate of interest to steady itself. Nevertheless in a period of rapidly changing prices, the money rate of interest seldom adjusts itself adequately or fast enough to prevent the real rate from becoming abnormal. For it is not the *fact* of a given rise of prices, but the *expectation* of a rise compounded of the various possible price-movements and the estimated probability of each, which affects money rates; and in countries where the currency has not collapsed completely, there has seldom or never existed a sufficient general confidence in a further rise or fall of prices to cause the short-money rate of interest to rise above 10 per cent per annum, or to fall below 1 per cent.[1] A fluctuation of this order is not sufficient to balance a movement of prices, up or down, of more than (say) 5 per cent per annum,—a rate which the actual price movement has frequently exceeded.

Germany has recently provided an illustration of the extraordinary degree in which the money rate of interest can rise in its endeavour to keep up with the real rate, when prices have continued to rise for so long and with such violence that, rightly or

---

[1] The merchant, who borrows money in order to take advantage of a prospective high real rate of interest, has to act in advance of the rise in prices, and is calculating on a probability, not upon a certainty, with the result that he will be deterred by a movement in the money rate of interest of much less magnitude than the contrary movement in the real rate of interest, upon which indeed he is reckoning, yet is not reckoning with certainty.

wrongly, every one believes that they will continue
to rise further. Yet even there the money rate of
interest has never risen high enough to keep pace
with the rise of prices. In the autumn of 1922,
the full effects were just becoming visible of the long
preceding period during which the real rate of interest
in Germany had reached a high negative figure, that
is to say during which any one who could borrow
marks and turn them into assets would have found
at the end of any given period that the appreciation
in the mark-value of the assets was far greater than
the interest he had to pay for borrowing them. By
this means great fortunes were snatched out of general
calamity ; and those made most who had seen first,
that the right game was to borrow and to borrow
and to borrow, and thus secure the difference between
the real rate of interest and the money rate. But
after this had been good business for many months,
every one began to take a hand, with belated results
on the money rate of interest. At that time, with a
nominal Reichsbank rate of 8 per cent, the effective
gilt-edged rate for short loans had risen to 22 per cent
per annum. During the first half of 1923, the rate of
the Reichsbank itself rose to 24 per cent, and sub-
sequently to 30, and finally 108 per cent, whilst the
market rate fluctuated violently at preposterous
figures, reaching at times 3 per cent *per week* for
certain types of loan. With the final currency
collapse of July-September 1923, the open market

rate was altogether demoralised, and reached figures of 100 per cent per month. In face, however, of the rate of currency depreciation, even such figures were inadequate, and the bold borrower was still making money.

In Hungary, Poland, and Russia—wherever prices were expected to collapse yet further—the same phenomenon was present, exhibiting as through a microscope what takes place everywhere when prices are expected to rise.

On the other hand, when prices are falling 30 to 40 per cent between the average of one year and that of the next, as they were in Great Britain and in the United States during 1921, even a bank rate of 1 per cent would have been oppressive to business, since it would have corresponded to a very high rate of real interest. Any one who could have foreseen the movement even partially would have done well for himself by selling out his assets and staying out of business for the time being.

But if the depreciation of money is a source of gain to the business man, it is also the occasion of opprobrium. To the consumer the business man's exceptional profits appear as the cause (instead of the consequence) of the hated rise of prices. Amidst the rapid fluctuations of his fortunes he himself loses his conservative instincts, and begins to think more of the large gains of the moment than of the lesser, but permanent, profits of normal business. The welfare of his enterprise in the relatively distant future weighs less with him than before, and thoughts are excited of a quick fortune and clearing out. His excessive gains have come to him unsought and without fault or design on his part, but once acquired he does not lightly surrender them, and will struggle to retain his booty. With such impulses and so placed, the business man is himself not free from a suppressed uneasiness. In his heart he loses his former self-confidence in his relation to society, in his utility and necessity in the economic scheme. He fears the future of his business and his class, and the less secure he feels his fortune to be the tighter he clings to it. The business man, the prop of society and the builder of the future, to whose activities and rewards there had been accorded, not long ago, an almost religious sanction, he of all men and classes most respectable, praiseworthy and necessary, with whom interference was not only disastrous but almost impious, was now to suffer sidelong glances, to feel himself suspected and attacked, the victim of unjust and injurious laws,—to become, and know himself half-guilty, a profiteer.

No man of spirit will consent to remain poor if he believes his betters to have gained their goods by lucky gambling. To convert the business man into the profiteer is to strike a blow at capitalism, because it destroys the psychological equilibrium

which permits the perpetuance of unequal rewards.
The economic doctrine of normal profits, vaguely
apprehended by every one, is a necessary condition
for the justification of capitalism.   The business
man is only tolerable so long as his gains can be
held to bear some relation to what, roughly and
in some sense, his activities have contributed to
society.

This, then, is the second disturbance to the
existing economic order for which the depreciation
of money is responsible.   If the fall in the value
of money discourages investment, it also discredits
enterprise.

Not that the business man was allowed, even
during the period of boom, to retain the whole of
his exceptional profits.   A host of popular remedies
vainly attempted to cure the evils of the day ; which
remedies themselves—subsidies, price and rent fixing,
profiteer hunting, and excess profits duties—eventually became not the least part of the evils.

In due course came the depression, with falling
prices, which operate on those who hold stocks in
a manner exactly opposite to rising prices.   Excessive
losses, bearing no relation to the efficiency of the
business, took the place of windfall gains ; and the
effort of every one to hold as small stocks as possible
brought industry to a standstill, just as previously
their efforts to accumulate stocks had over-stimulated
it.   Unemployment succeeded Profiteering as the

problem of the hour. But whilst the cyclical movement of trade and credit has, in the good-currency
countries, partly reversed, for the time being at least,
the great rise of 1920, it has, in the countries of continuing inflation, made no more than a ripple on the
rapids of depreciation.

3. *The Earner.*

It has been a commonplace of economic text-books
that wages tend to lag behind prices, with the result
that the real earnings of the wage-earner are diminished during a period of rising prices. This has often
been true in the past, and may be true even now of
certain classes of labour which are ill-placed or ill-
organised for improving their position. But in Great
Britain, at any rate, and in the United States also,
some important sections of labour were able to take
advantage of the situation not only to obtain money
wages equivalent in purchasing power to what they
had before, but to secure a real improvement, to
combine this with a diminution in their hours of work
(and, so far, of the work done), and to accomplish
this (in the case of Great Britain) at a time when the
total wealth of the community as a whole had suffered
a decrease. This reversal of the usual course has not
been due to an accident and is traceable to definite
causes.

The organisation of certain classes of labour—
railwaymen, miners, dockers, and others—for the

purpose of securing wage increases is better than it was. Life in the army, perhaps for the first time in the history of wars, raised in many respects the conventional standard of requirements,—the soldier was better clothed, better shod, and often better fed than the labourer, and his wife, adding in war time a separation allowance to new opportunities to earn, had also enlarged her ideas.

But these influences, while they would have supplied the motive, might have lacked the means to the result if it had not been for another factor— the windfalls of the profiteer. The fact that the business man had been gaining, and gaining notoriously, considerable windfall profits in excess of the normal profits of trade, laid him open to pressure, not only from his employees but from public opinion generally ; and enabled him to meet this pressure without financial difficulty. In fact, it was worth his while to pay ransom, and to share with his workmen the good fortune of the day.

Thus the working classes improved their *relative* position in the years following the war, as against all other classes except that of the "profiteers." In some important cases they improved their absolute position—that is to say, account being taken of shorter hours, increased money wages, and higher prices, some sections of the working classes secured for themselves a higher real remuneration for each unit of effort or work done. But we cannot estimate

the *stability* of this state of affairs, as contrasted with
its desirability, unless we know the source from which
the increased reward of the working classes was
drawn. Was it due to a permanent modification of
the economic factors which determine the distribution of the national product between different classes ?
Or was it due to some temporary and exhaustible
influence connected with inflation and with the resulting disturbance in the standard of value ?

A violent disturbance of the standard of value
obscures the true situation, and for a time one class
can benefit at the expense of another surreptitiously
and without producing immediately the inevitable
reaction. In such conditions a country can without
knowing it expend in current consumption those
savings which it thinks it is investing for the future ;
and it can even trench on existing capital or fail
to make good its current depreciation. When the
value of money is greatly fluctuating, the distinction between capital and income becomes confused.
It is one of the evils of a depreciating currency
that it enables a community to live on its capital
unawares. The increasing *money* value of the community's capital goods obscures temporarily a diminution in the real quantity of the stock.

The period of depression has exacted its penalty
from the working classes more in the form of unemployment than by a lowering of real wages, and
State assistance to the unemployed has greatly

moderated even this penalty. Money wages have followed prices downwards. But the depression of 1921–22 did not reverse or even greatly diminish the relative advantage gained by the working classes over the middle class during the previous years. In 1923 British wage rates stood at an appreciably higher level above the pre-war rates than did the cost of living, if allowance is made for the shorter hours worked.

In Germany and Austria also, but in a far greater degree than in England or in France, the change in the value of money has thrown the burden of hard circumstances on the middle class, and hitherto the labouring class have by no means supported their full proportionate share.   If it be true that university professors in Germany have some responsibility for the atmosphere which bred war, their class has paid the penalty. The effects of the impoverishment, throughout Europe, of the middle class, out of which most good things have sprung, must slowly accumulate in a decay of Science and Art.

We conclude that Inflation redistributes wealth in a manner very injurious to the investor, very beneficial to the business man, and probably, in modern industrial conditions, beneficial on the whole to the earner.   Its most striking consequence is its *injustice* to those who in good faith have committed their savings to titles to money rather than to things. But injustice on such a scale has further consequences. The above discussion suggests that the diminution in the production of wealth which has taken place in Europe since the war has been, to a certain extent, at the expense, not of the consumption of any class, but of the accumulation of capital. Moreover, Inflation has not only diminished the capacity of the investing class to save but has destroyed the atmosphere of confidence which is a condition of the willingness to save. Yet a growing population requires, for the maintenance of the same standard of life, a proportionate growth of capital. In Great Britain for many years to come, regardless of what the birth-rate may be from now onwards (and at the present time the number of births per day is nearly double the number of deaths), upwards of 250,000 new labourers will enter the labour market annually in excess of those going out of it. To maintain this growing body of labour at the same standard of life as before, we require not merely growing markets but a growing capital equipment. In order to keep our standards from deterioration, the national capital must grow as fast as the national labour supply, which means new savings of at least £250,000,000 [1] per annum at present.

---

[1] That is to say, it costs not less than £1000 in new capital outlay to equip a working man with organisation and appliances, which will render his labour efficient, and to house and supply himself and his family. Indeed this is probably an underestimate.

The favourable conditions for saving which existed in the nineteenth century, even though we smile at them, provided a proportionate growth between capital and population. The disturbance of the pre-existing balance between classes, which in its origins is largely traceable to the changes in the value of money, may have destroyed these favourable conditions.

On the other hand Deflation, as we shall see in the second section of the next chapter, is liable, in these days of huge national debts expressed in legal-tender money, to overturn the balance so far the other way in the interests of the *rentier*, that the burden of taxation becomes intolerable on the productive classes of the community.

II.—CHANGES IN THE VALUE OF MONEY, AS AFFECTING PRODUCTION.

If, for any reason right or wrong, the business world *expects* that prices will fall, the processes of production tend to be inhibited ; and if it expects that prices will rise, they tend to be over-stimulated. A fluctuation in the measuring-rod of value does not alter in the least the wealth of the world, the needs of the world, or the productive capacity of the world. It ought not, therefore, to affect the character or the volume of what is produced. A movement of *relative* prices, that is to say of the comparative prices of different commodities, *ought* to influence the character of production, because it is an indication that various commodities are not being produced in the exactly right proportions.   But this is not true of a change, as such, in the *general* price level.

The fact that the expectation of changes in the *general* price level affects the processes of production, is deeply rooted in the peculiarities of the existing economic organisation of society, partly in those described in the preceding sections of this chapter, partly in others to be mentioned in a moment.   We have already seen that a change in the general level of prices, that is to say a change in the measuring-rod, which fixes the obligation of the borrowers of money (who make the decisions which set production in motion) to the lenders (who are inactive once they have lent their money), effects a redistribution of real wealth between the two groups.   Furthermore, the active group can, if they foresee such a change, alter their action in advance in such a way as to minimise their losses to the other group or to increase their gains from it, if and when the expected change in the value of money occurs.   If they expect a fall, it may pay them, as a group, to damp production down, although such enforced idleness impoverishes society as a whole.   If they expect a rise, it may pay them to increase their borrowings and to swell production beyond the point where the real return is just sufficient to recompense society as a whole for the effort made.

Sometimes, of course, a change in the measuring-rod, especially if it is unforeseen, may benefit one group at the expense of the other disproportionately to any influence it exerts on the volume of production ; but the tendency, in so far as the active group anticipate a change, will be as I have described it.[1] This is simply to say that the intensity of production is largely governed in existing conditions by the anticipated real profit of the *entrepreneur.* Yet this criterion is the right one for the community as a whole only when the delicate adjustment of interests is not upset by fluctuations in the standard of value.

But there is a further reason, connected with the above but nevertheless distinct, why modern methods of production require a stable standard,— a reason springing to a certain extent out of the character of the social organisation described above, but aggravated by the technical methods of present-day productive processes. With the development of international trade, involving great distances between

---

[1] The interests of the salaried and wage-earning classes will, in so far as their salaries and wages tend to be steadier in money-value than in real-value, coincide with those of the inactive capitalist group. The interests of the consumer will, in so far as he can vary the distribution of his floating resources between cash and goods purchased in advance of consumption, coincide with those of the active capitalist group ; and his decisions, made in his own interests, may serve to reinforce the effect of those of the latter. But that the interests of the same individual will often be those of one of the groups in one of his capacities and of the other in another of his capacities, does not save the situation or affect the argument. For his losses in one capacity depend only infinitesimally on him personally refraining from action in his other capacity. The facts, that a man is a cannibal at home and eaten abroad, do not cancel out to render him innocuous and safe.

the place of original production and the place of final consumption, and with the increased complication of the technical processes of manufacture, the amount of *risk* which attaches to the undertaking of production and the length of time through which this risk must be carried are much greater than they would be in a comparatively small self-contained community. Even in agriculture, whilst the risk to the consumer is diminished by drawing supplies from many different sources, which average the fluctuations of the seasons, the risk to the agricultural producer is increased, since, when his crop falls below his expectations in volume, he may fail to be compensated by a higher price. This increased risk is the price which producers have to pay for the other advantages of a high degree of specialisation and for the variety of their markets and their sources of supply.

The provision of adequate facilities for the carrying of this risk at a moderate cost is one of the greatest of the problems of modern economic life, and one of those which so far have been least satisfactorily solved. The business of keeping the productive machine in continuous operation (and thereby avoiding unemployment) would be greatly simplified if this risk could be diminished or if we could devise a better means of insurance against it for the individual *entrepreneur*.

A considerable part of the risk arises out of fluctuations in the *relative* value of a commodity compared with that of commodities in general during the interval which must elapse between the commencement of production and the time of consumption. This part of the risk is independent of the vagaries of money, and must be tackled by methods with which we are not concerned here. But there is also a considerable risk directly arising out of instability in the value of money. During the lengthy process of production the business world is incurring outgoings in terms of *money*—paying out in money for wages and other expenses of production—in the expectation of recouping this outlay by disposing of the product for *money* at a later date. That is to say, the business world as a whole must always be in a position where it stands to gain by a rise of price and to lose by a fall of price. Whether it likes it or not, the technique of production under a *régime* of money-contract forces the business world always to carry a big speculative position ; and if it is reluctant to carry this position, the productive process must be slackened. The argument is not affected by the fact that there is some degree of specialisation of function within the business world, in so far as the professional speculator comes to the assistance of the producer proper by taking over from him a part of his risk.

Now it follows from this, not merely that the *actual occurrence* of price changes profits some classes and injures others (which has been the theme of the first section of this chapter), but that a *general fear* of falling prices may inhibit the productive process altogether. For if prices are expected to fall, not enough risk-takers can be found who are willing to carry a speculative " bull " position, and this means that *entrepreneurs* will be reluctant to embark on lengthy productive processes involving a money outlay long in advance of money recoupment,—whence unemployment. The *fact* of falling prices injures *entrepreneurs* ; consequently the *fear* of falling prices causes them to protect themselves by curtailing their operations ; yet it is upon the aggregate of their individual estimations of the risk, and their willingness to run the risk, that the activity of production and of employment mainly depends.

There is a further aggravation of the case, in that an expectation about the course of prices tends, if it is widely held, to be cumulative in its results up to a certain point. If prices are expected to rise and the business world acts on this expectation, that very fact causes them to rise for a time and, by verifying the expectation, reinforces it ; and similarly, if it expects them to fall. Thus a comparatively weak initial impetus may be adequate to produce a considerable fluctuation.

Three generations of economists have recognised that certain influences produce a progressive and continuing change in the value of money, that others produce in it an oscillatory movement, and that the latter act cumulatively in their initial stages but produce the conditions for a reaction after a certain point. But their investigations into the oscillatory movements have been chiefly confined, until lately, to the question what kind of cause is responsible for the initial impetus. Some have been fascinated by the idea that the initial cause is always the same and is astronomically regular in the times of its appearance. Others have maintained, more plausibly, that sometimes one thing operates and sometimes another.

It is one of the objects of this book to urge that the best way to cure this mortal disease of individualism is to provide that there shall never exist any confident expectation either that prices generally are going to fall or that they are going to rise ; and also that there shall be no serious risk that a movement, if it does occur, will be a big one. If, unexpectedly and accidentally, a moderate movement were to occur, wealth, though it might be redistributed, would not be diminished thereby.

To procure this result by removing all possible influences towards an initial movement, whether such influences are to be found in the skies only or everywhere, would seem to be a hopeless enterprise. The remedy would lie, rather, in so controlling the standard of value that, whenever something occurred which, left to itself, would create an expectation of a change in the general level of prices, the controlling authority should take steps to counteract this expectation by setting in motion some factor of a contrary tendency. Even if such a policy were not wholly successful, either in counteracting expectations or in avoiding actual movements, it would be an improvement on the policy of sitting quietly by, whilst a standard of value, governed by chance causes and deliberately removed from central control, produces expectations which paralyse or intoxicate the government of production.

We see, therefore, that rising prices and falling prices each have their characteristic disadvantage. The Inflation which causes the former means Injustice to individuals and to classes,—particularly to investors ; and is therefore unfavourable to saving. The Deflation which causes falling prices means Impoverishment to labour and to enterprise by leading *entrepreneurs* to restrict production, in their endeavour to avoid loss to themselves ; and is therefore disastrous to employment. The counterparts are, of course, also true,—namely that Deflation means Injustice to borrowers, and that Inflation leads to the over-stimulation of industrial activity. But these results are not so marked as those emphasised above, because borrowers are in a better position to protect themselves from the worst effects of Deflation than lenders are to protect themselves from those of Inflation, and because labour is in a better position to protect itself from over-exertion in good times than from under-employment in bad times.

Thus Inflation is unjust and Deflation is inexpedient. Of the two perhaps Deflation is, if we rule out exaggerated inflations such as that of Germany, the worse ; because it is worse, in an impoverished world, to provoke unemployment than to disappoint the *rentier*. But it is not necessary that we should weigh one evil against the other. It is easier to agree that both are evils to be shunned. The Individualistic Capitalism of to-day, precisely because it entrusts saving to the individual investor and production to the individual employer, *presumes* a stable measuring-rod of value, and cannot be efficient —perhaps cannot survive—without one.

For these grave causes we must free ourselves from the deep distrust which exists against allowing the regulation of the standard of value to be the subject of *deliberate decision*. We can no longer afford to leave it in the category of which the distinguishing characteristics are possessed in different degrees by the weather, the birth-rate, and the Constitution,—matters which are settled by natural causes, or are the resultant of the separate action of many individuals acting independently, or require a Revolution to change them.

CHAPTER II

I. *Inflation as a Method of Taxation*

A GOVERNMENT can live for a long time, even the German Government or the Russian Government, by printing paper money. That is to say, it can by this means secure the command over real resources,—resources just as real as those obtained by taxation. The method is condemned, but its efficacy, up to a point, must be admitted. A Government can live by this means when it can live by no other. It is the form of taxation which the public find hardest to evade and even the weakest Government can enforce, when it can enforce nothing else. Of this character have been the progressive and catastrophic inflations practised in Central and Eastern Europe, as distinguished from the limited and oscillatory inflations, experienced for example in Great Britain and the United States, which have been examined in the preceding chapter.

The Quantity Theory of Money states that the

41

amount of cash which the community requires, *assuming certain habits of business and of banking to be established*, and assuming also a given level and distribution of wealth, depends on the level of prices. If the consumption and production of actual goods are unaltered but prices and wages are doubled, then twice as much cash as before is required to do the business. The truth of this, properly explained and qualified, it is foolish to deny. The Theory infers from this that the *aggregate real value* of all the paper money in circulation remains more or less the same, irrespective of the *number of units* of it in circulation, provided the habits and prosperity of the people are not changed,—*i.e.* the community retains in the shape of cash the command over a more or less constant amount of real wealth, which is the same thing as to say that the total quantity of money in circulation has a more or less fixed purchasing power.[1]

Let us suppose that there are in circulation 9,000,000 currency notes, and that they have altogether a value equivalent to 36,000,000 gold dollars.[2] Suppose that the Government prints a further 3,000,000 notes, so that the amount of currency is now 12,000,000 ; then, in accordance with the above theory, the 12,000,000 notes are still

---

[1] See also Chapter III., Section I.

[2] It will simplify the argument to ignore the fact that the value of gold in terms of commodities is itself a fluctuating one, and to treat the value of a currency in terms of gold as a rough measure of its value in terms of " real resources " generally.

only equivalent to \$36,000,000. In the first state of affairs, therefore, each note = \$4, and in the second state of affairs each note = \$3. Consequently the 9,000,000 notes originally held by the public are now worth \$27,000,000 instead of \$36,000,000, and the 3,000,000 notes newly issued by the Government are worth \$9,000,000. Thus by the process of printing the additional notes the Government has transferred from the public to itself an amount of resources equal to \$9,000,000, just as successfully as if it had raised this sum in taxation.

On whom has the tax fallen ? Clearly on the holders of the original 9,000,000 notes, whose notes are now worth 25 per cent less than they were before. The inflation has amounted to a tax of 25 per cent on all holders of notes in proportion to their holdings. The burden of the tax is well spread, cannot be evaded, costs nothing to collect, and falls, in a rough sort of way, in proportion to the wealth of the victim. No wonder its superficial advantages have attracted Ministers of Finance.

Temporarily, the yield of the tax is even a little better for the Government than by the above calculation. For the new notes can be passed off at first at the same value as though there were still only 9,000,000 notes altogether. It is only after the new notes get into circulation and people begin to spend them that they realise that the notes are worth less than before.

What is there to prevent the Government from repeating this process over and over again ? The reader must observe that the aggregate note issue is still worth $36,000,000. If, therefore, the Government now prints a further 4,000,000 notes, there will be 16,000,000 notes altogether, which by the same argument as before are worth $2.25 each instead of $3, and by issuing the 4,000,000 notes the Government has, just as before, transferred an amount of resources equal to $9,000,000 from the public to itself. The holders of notes have again suffered a tax of 25 per cent in proportion to their holdings.

Like other forms of taxation, these exactions, if overdone and out of proportion to the wealth of the community, must diminish its prosperity and lower its standards, so that at the lower standard of life the aggregate value of the currency may fall and still be enough to go round. But this effect cannot interfere very much with the efficacy of taxing by inflation. Even if the aggregate real value of the currency falls for these reasons to a half or two-thirds of what it was before, which represents a tremendous lowering of the standards of life, this only means that the quantity of notes which the Government must issue in order to obtain a given result must be raised proportionately. It remains true that by this means the Government can still secure for itself a large share of the available surplus of the community.

Has the public in the last resort no remedy, no means of protecting itself against these ingenious depredations ?   It has only one remedy,—to change its habits in the use of money.   The initial assumption on which our argument rested was that the community did *not* change its habits in the use of money.

Experience shows that the public generally is very slow to grasp the situation and embrace the remedy.   Indeed, at first there may be a change of habit in the wrong direction, which actually facilitates the Government's operations.   The public is so much accustomed to thinking of money as the ultimate standard, that, when prices begin to rise, believing that the rise must be temporary, they tend to hoard their money and to postpone purchases, with the result that they hold in monetary form a *larger* aggregate of real value than before.   And, similarly, when the fall in the real value of the money is reflected in the exchanges, foreigners, thinking that the fall is abnormal and temporary, purchase the money for the purpose of hoarding it.

But sooner or later the second phase sets in. The public discover that it is the holders of notes who suffer taxation and defray the expenses of government, and they begin to change their habits and to economise in their holding of notes.   They can do this in various ways :—(1) instead of keeping some part of their ultimate reserves in money they can spend this money on durable objects, jewellery or household goods, and keep their reserves in this form instead ; (2) they can reduce the amount of till-money and pocket-money that they keep and the average length of time for which they keep it,[1] even at the cost of great personal inconvenience ; and (3) they can employ foreign money in many transactions where it would have been more natural and convenient to use their own.

By these means they can get along and do their business with an amount of notes having an aggregate real value substantially less than before. For example, the notes in circulation become worth altogether $20,000,000 instead of $36,000,000, with the result that the next inflationary levy by the Government, falling on a smaller amount, must be at a greater rate in order to yield a given sum.

When the public take alarm faster than they can change their habits, and, in their efforts to avoid loss, run down the amount of real resources, which they hold in the form of money, *below* the work-

---

[1] In Moscow the unwillingness to hold money except for the shortest possible time reached at one period a fantastic intensity. If a grocer sold a pound of cheese, he ran off with the roubles as fast as his legs could carry him to the Central Market to replenish his stocks by changing them into cheese again, lest they lost their value before he got there ; thus justifying the prevision of economists in naming the phenomenon " velocity of circulation " ! In Vienna, during the period of collapse, mushroom exchange banks sprang up at every street corner, where you could change your krone into Zurich francs within a few minutes of receiving them, and so avoid the risk of loss during the time it would take you to reach your usual bank. It became a seasonable witticism to allege that a prudent man at a café ordering a bock of beer should order a second bock at the same time, even at the expense of drinking it tepid, lest the price should rise meanwhile.

II PUBLIC FINANCE AND THE VALUE OF MONEY   47

ing minimum, seeking to supply their daily needs
for cash by borrowing, they get penalised, as in
Germany in 1923, by prodigious rates of money-
interest. The rates rise, as we have seen in the
previous chapter, until the rate of interest on money
equals or exceeds the anticipated rate of the depreciation of money. Indeed it is always likely, when
money is rapidly depreciating, that there will be recurrent periods of scarcity of currency, because the
public, in their anxiety not to hold too much money,
will fail to provide themselves even with the minimum
which they will require in practice.

Whilst economists have sometimes described these
phenomena in terms of an increase in the velocity of
circulation due to loss of confidence in the currency ;
nevertheless there are not, I think, many passages
in economic literature where the matter is clearly
analysed. Professor Cannan's article on " The Application of the Apparatus of Supply and Demand to
Units of Currency " (Economic Journal, December
1921) is one of the most noteworthy. He points out
that the common assumption that " the elasticity of
demand for money is unity " is equivalent to the
assertion that a mere variation in the quantity of
money does not affect the willingness and habits of
the public as holders of purchasing power in that
form. But in extreme cases this assumption does
not hold ; for if it did, there would be no limit to
the sums which the Government could extract from

the public by means of inflation. It is, therefore, unsafe to assume that the elasticity of demand is necessarily unity. Professor Lehfeldt followed this up in a subsequent issue of the *Economic Journal* (December 1922) by a calculation of the actual elasticity of demand for money in some recent instances. He found that between July 1920 and April 1922, the elasticity of demand for money fell to an average of about ·73 in Austria, ·67 in Poland, and ·5 in Germany. Thus in the last stages of inflation the prodigious increase in the velocity of circulation may have as much, or more, effect in raising prices and depreciating the exchanges than the increase in the volume of notes. The note-issuing authorities often cry out against what they regard as the unfair and anomalous fact of the notes falling in value *more* than in proportion to their increased volume. Yet it is nothing of the kind ; it is merely the result of the one method to evade a crushing burden left open to the public, who discover for themselves, sooner than the financiers, that the law of unit elasticity in their demand for money can be escaped.

Nevertheless, it is evident that so long as the public use money at all, the Government can continue to raise resources by inflation. Moreover, the conveniences of using money in daily life are so great that the public are prepared, rather than forego them, to pay the inflationary tax, provided it is not raised to a prohibitive level. Like other conveniences of life the use of money is taxable, and, although for various reasons this particular form of taxation is highly inexpedient, a Government can get resources by a *continuous* practice of inflation, even when this is foreseen by the public generally, unless the sums they seek to raise in this way are very grossly excessive. Just as a toll can be levied on the use of roads or a turnover tax on business transactions, so also on the use of money. The higher the toll and the tax, the less traffic on the roads, and the less business transacted, so also the less money carried. But some traffic is so indispensable, some business so profitable, some money-payments so convenient, that only a very high levy will stop completely all traffic, all business, all payments. A Government has to remember, however, that even if a tax is not prohibitive it may be unprofitable, and that a medium, rather than an extreme, imposition will yield the greatest gain.

Suppose that the rate of inflation is such that the value of the money falls by half every year, and suppose that the cash used by the public for retail purchases in shops is turned over 100 times a year (*i.e.* stays in one pocket for half a week on the average) ; then this is only equivalent to a turnover tax of $\frac{1}{2}$ per cent on each transaction. The public will gladly pay such a tax rather than suffer the trouble and inconvenience of barter with trams and tradesmen. Even if the value of the money falls by half every month, the public, by keeping their pocket-money so low that they turn it over once a day on the average instead of only twice a week, can still keep the tax down to the equivalent of less than 2 per cent on each transaction, or more precisely 4d. in the £. Even such a terrific rate of depreciation as this is not sufficient, therefore, to counterbalance the advantages of using money rather than barter in the trifling business of daily life. This is the explanation why, even in Germany and in Russia, the Government's notes remained current for many retail transactions.

For certain other purposes, however, to which money is put in a modern community, the inflationary tax becomes prohibitive at a much earlier stage. As a store of value, for example, money is rapidly discarded, as soon as further depreciation is confidently anticipated. As a unit of account, for contracts and for balance sheets, it quickly becomes worse than useless, although for such purposes the privilege of the current money as legal-tender for the discharge of debts stands in the way of its being discarded as soon as it ought to be.

In the last phase, when the use of the legal-tender money has been discarded for all purposes except trifling out-of-pocket expenditure, inflationary taxation has at last defeated itself. For in that case the total value of the note issue, which is sufficient to meet the public's minimum requirements, amounts to

a figure relatively so trifling that the amount of resources which the government can hope to raise by
yet further inflation—without pushing it to a point at
which the money will be discarded even for out-of-
pocket trifles—is correspondingly small.   Thus at last,
unless it is employed with some measure of moderation, this potent instrument of governmental exaction
breaks in the hands of those that use it, and leaves
them at the same time with the rest of their fiscal
system in total ruins ;—out of which, in the ebb and
flow of the economic life of nations, may emerge
once more a reformed and admirable system.   The
chervonetz of Moscow and the krone of Vienna are
already stabler units than the franc or the lira.

All these matters can be illustrated from the recent
experiences of Germany, Austria, and Russia.   The
following tables show the gold value of the note issues
of these countries at various dates :

GERMANY.	Volume of Note Issue in Milliard Paper Marks.	Number of Paper Marks = 1 Gold Mark.	Value of Note Issue in Milliard Gold Marks.
December 1920 . .	81	17	4·8
December 1921 . .	122	46	2·7
March 1922 . . .	140	65	2·2
June 1922 . . .	180	90	2·0
September 1922 . .	331	349	0·9
December 1922 . .	1,293	1,778	0·7
February 1923 . .	2,266	11,200	0·2
March 1923 . . .	4,956	4,950	1·0
June 1923 . . .	17,000	45,000	0·4
August 1923 . . .	116,000	1,000,000	0·116

AUSTRIA.	Volume of Note Issue in Milliard Paper Krone.	Number of Paper Krone = 1 Gold Krone.	Value of Note Issue in Million Gold Krone.
June 1920 . . .	17	27	620
December 1920 . .	30	70	430
December 1921 . .	174	533	326
March 1922 . . .	304	1,328	229
June 1922 . . .	550	2,911	189
September 1922 . .	2,278	14,473	157
December 1922 . .	4,080	14,473	282
March 1923 . . .	4,238	14,363	295
August 1923 . . .	5,557	14,369	387

RUSSIA.	Volume of Note Issue in Milliard Paper Roubles.	Number of Paper Roubles * = 1 Gold Rouble.	Value of Note Issue in Million Gold Roubles.
January 1919 . . .	61	103	592
January 1920 . . .	225	1,670	134
January 1921 . . .	1,169	26,000	45
January 1922 . . .	17,539	172,000	102 †
March 1922 . . .	48,535	1,060,000	46
May 1922 . . .	145,635	3,800,000	38 ‡
July 1922 . . .	320,497	4,102,000	78
October 1922 . . .	815,486	6,964,000	117
January 1923 . . .	2,138,711	15,790,000	135
June 1923 . . .	8,050,000	97,690,000	82 §

* " Gosplan " figures for 1923, Moscow Economic Institute figures previously.

† The increase is due to the reintroduction of the use of money in State transactions as a result of the New Economic Policy.

‡ Lowest point reached.

§ The decrease may be attributed to the introduction of the chervonetz (see p. 57 below).

The characteristics of each phase emerge clearly. The tables show, first of all, how quickly, during the period of collapse, the rate of the depreciation of the value of the money outstrips the rate of the inflation of its volume. During the collapse of the German mark beginning with December 1920, the rate of depreciation proceeded for some time roughly twice as fast as that of the inflation, and eventually by June 1923, when the volume of the note-issue had increased 200-fold compared with December 1920, the value of a paper mark had fallen 2500-fold. The figures given above for Austria begin at a rather later stage of the *débâcle*. But if we equate Austria in June 1920 to Germany in December 1920, the progress of events between that date and September 1922 is roughly comparable to that in Germany between December 1920 and May 1923. The figures for Russia between January 1919 and the early part of 1923 also exhibit the same general features.

These tables all commence after a considerable depreciation had already occurred and the gold-value of the aggregate note-issue had fallen considerably below the normal.[1] Nevertheless their earliest entries still belong to the period when an eventual recovery was still widely anticipated and the general public had not at all appreciated what they were in for. They indicate that as the situation develops from this point onwards and the use of money is discarded except for retail transactions, the aggregate value of the note-issue falls by about four-fifths. As the result

---

[1] The pre-war currency of Germany was estimated at about 6 milliard gold marks (£300,000,000), or nearly £5 per head.

SCCCC - LIBRARY
WITHDRAWN
St. Peters, MO 63376

of extreme panic or depression a further fall may
occur for a time ; but, unless the money is discarded
altogether, a minimum is reached eventually from
which the least favourable circumstance will cause a
sharp recovery.

The temporary recovery in Germany after the
collapse of February 1923 exhibited how a point may
come when, if the money is to continue in use at all,
a bottom is reached and a technical position is created
in which some recovery is possible. When the gold
value of the currency has fallen to a very low figure,
it is easy for the Government, if it has any external
resources at all, to give sufficient support to prevent
the exchange from falling further for the time being.
And since by that time the public will have carried
their attempts to economise the use of money to a
pitch of inconvenience which it is impracticable to
continue, even a moderate weakening in the degree
of their distrust of the future value of the money
will lead to some increase in their use of it ; with the
result that the aggregate value of the note issue will
tend to recover. By February 1923 these conditions
existed in Germany in a high degree. The German
Government was able within two months, in the face
of most adverse political conditions, to double the
exchange-value of the mark whilst simultaneously
more than doubling the note circulation. Even so
the gold value of the note issue was only brought
back to what it had been six months earlier ; and if

even a moderate degree of confidence had been restored, it might have been possible to bring the value of the note circulation of Germany up to (say) 2 milliard gold marks (£100,000,000) at least, which is probably about the lowest figure at which it can stand permanently, unless every one is to put himself to intolerable inconvenience in his efforts to hold as little money as possible. Incidentally the Government is able during the period of recovery to obtain, once more, through the issue of notes the command over a considerable amount of real resources.

In Austria, where, at the date of writing, the exchange has been stabilised for a year, the same phenomenon has been apparent with the growth of confidence, the gold value of the note issue having been raised to nearly two and a half times the low point reached in September 1922. The fact of stabilisation, with foreign aid, has, by increasing confidence, permitted this increase of the note issue without imperilling the stabilisation, and will probably permit in course of time a substantial further increase.

Even in Russia a sort of equilibrium seems to have been reached. There the last phase had appeared by the middle of 1922, when a tenfold inflation in six months [1] had brought the aggregate value of the note issue below £4,000,000, which clearly could not

---

[1] Recent experience everywhere seems to show that it is possible to inflate 100 per cent every three months without entirely killing the use of money in retail transactions, but that a greater rate of inflation than this can only be indulged in at the peril of total collapse.

be adequate for the transaction of the business of
Russia even in its present condition. A point had
been reached when the use of paper roubles was
being dispensed with altogether. At about that date
I had the opportunity of discussion at Genoa with
some of the Soviet financiers. They have always
been more self-conscious and deliberate than others
in their monetary policy. They maintained at that
time that, with the help of legal compulsion to employ
paper roubles for certain types of transaction, these
roubles could always be maintained in circulation up
to a certain *minimum* real value, however certain the
public might be as to their ultimate worthlessness.
According to this calculation, it would always be
possible to raise (say) £3,000,000 to £4,000,000 per
annum by this method, even though the paper rouble
regularly fell in value at the rate of a tenfold or a
hundredfold a year (one or more noughts being
struck off the monetary unit annually for convenience
of calculation). During the year following they did,
in fact, decidedly better than this, and, by reducing
the rate of inflation to a figure not much in excess of
100 per cent per three months, were able to raise the
aggregate value of the note issue to more than double
the lowest point reached. The equivalent of something like £15,000,000 seems to have been raised
during the year (April 1922–April 1923) by this means
towards the expenses of government, at the cost of
having to strike only one nought off the monetary

unit for the whole year ![1]   At the same time, in order
to furnish a reliable store of value and a basis for
foreign trade, the Soviet Government introduced in
December 1922 a new currency unit (the chervonetz,
or gold ducat), freely convertible on sterling-exchange
standard principles, alongside the paper rouble, which
was still indispensable as an instrument of taxation.
So far this new bank note has kept respectable.
By August 1923 its circulation had risen to nearly
16,000,000 having a value of about £16,000,000, and
its exchange value had kept steady, the State Bank
undertaking to convert the chervonetz on a parity
with the £ sterling.[2]   Thus by the middle of 1923 the
aggregate value of the Russian note issues, good and
bad money together, had risen to the substantial figure
of £25,000,000, as compared with barely £4,000,000
at the date of the Genoa Conference in May 1922,
thus indicating the return of confidence and the

[1] The Soviet Government have always regarded monetary inflation
quite frankly as an instrument of taxation, and have themselves calculated
that the purchasing power secured to the State by this means has amounted
in the past to the following sums :

1918	.	.	.	.	.	525 million gold roubles
1919	.	.	.	.	.	380 ,, ,, ,,
1920	.	.	.	.	.	186 ,, ,, ,,
1921	.	.	.	.	.	143 ,, ,, ,,
1922 (Jan. to March)	.	.	58 ,, ,, ,,

or (say) £130,000,000 altogether.

[2] So far the chervonetz has generally sold at a small premium, the
rates being :

March 15, 1923	.	.	.	.	.	ch. 1 = £1·07
April 17, 1923	.	.	.	.	.	ch. 1 = £1·05
June 15, 1923	.	.	.	.	.	ch. 1 = £0·94
July 27, 1923	.	.	.	.	.	ch. 1 = £1·05

re-inauguration of a monetary *régime*. Russia provides
an instructive example (at least for the moment) of
a sound money for substantial transactions alongside
small change for daily life, the progressive depreciation on which merely represents a quite supportable
rate of turn-over tax.

The collapse of the currency in Germany which
was the chief contributory cause to the fall of Dr.
Cuno's Government in August 1923, was due, not so
much to taxing by inflation—for that had been going
on for years—as to an increase in the *rate* of inflation
to a level almost prohibitive for daily transactions
and quite destructive of the legal-tender money as a
unit of account. We have seen that what concerns
the use of money in the retail transactions of daily
life is the *rate* of depreciation, rather than the absolute
amount of depreciation as compared with some
earlier date.

In the middle of 1922 I estimated, very roughly,
that the German Government had then been obtaining for some time past the equivalent of something
between £75,000,000 and £100,000,000 per annum by
means of printing money. Up to that time, however, a substantial proportion of these receipts had
been contributed through the purchase of mark-notes
by speculative foreigners. Nevertheless the German
public itself had probably paid upwards of £50,000,000
per annum in this form of taxation. Since the
German note issue was still worth £240,000,000 so

lately as December 1920 (see the table on p. 51) and had not fallen below £100,000,000 even in the middle of 1922, the rate of depreciation represented by the above, whilst sufficiently disastrous to the mark as a store of value or as a unit of account, had been by no means prohibitive to its continued use in daily life. In the latter half of 1922, however, the public learnt to make enough further economies in the use of the mark as money to reduce the value of the total note issue to about £60,000,000. The first effect of the Ruhr occupation was, as we have seen above (p. 54), to bring down the note issue below the minimum to which the public could adjust their habits, which resulted in the temporary recovery of March 1923. Nevertheless by the middle of 1923 the public was able to get along with a note issue worth about £20,000,000. All this time the German Government had continued to raise resources equivalent to round about £1,000,000 a week by note-printing— which meant a depreciation of 5 per cent a week even if the public had been unable to reduce any further the value of the aggregate note issue, and came in practice to about 10 per cent a week allowing for their yet further economies in the use of mark-currency.

But the expenses of the Ruhr resistance, coupled with the complete breakdown of other sources of taxation, had led, by May and June 1923, to the Government's raising the equivalent of, first, £2,000,000 and then £3,000,000 a week by note-printing. On a note issue, of which the total value had sunk by that time to about £20,000,000, this was pushing inflationary taxation to a preposterous and suicidal point. The social disorganisation, resulting from a rapid movement to do without the mark altogether, quickly resulted in Dr. Cuno's fall.[1] The climax was reached when, in Dr. Cuno's last days, the Government doubled the note issue in a week and raised the equivalent of £3,000,000 in that period out of a note issue worth about £4,000,000 altogether,—a performance far transcending the wildest extravagances of the Soviet.

By the time this book is published, Dr. Cuno's successors may have solved, or failed to solve, the problem facing them. However this may be, the restoration of a serviceable unit of account seems to be the first step. This is a necessary preliminary to the escape of the German financial system from the vicious circle in which it now moves. The Government cannot introduce a sound money, because, in

---

[1] It is necessary to admit that Dr. Cuno's failure to control incompetence at the Treasury and at the Reichsbank was bound to bring this about. During this catastrophic period those responsible for the financial policy of Germany did not do a single wise thing, or show the least appreciation of what was happening. The profits of note-printing were not even monopolised by the Government, and Herr Havenstein continued to allow the German banks to share in them, by discounting their bills at the Reichsbank at a rate of discount far below the rate of depreciation. Only at the end of August 1923 did the Reichsbank begin to require that borrowers should make good on repayment a percentage of the loss due to the depreciation of the borrowed marks (as reckoned by the dollar exchange) during the currency of the loan.

the absence of other revenue, the printing of an unsound money is the only way by which it can live. Yet a serviceable unit of account is a pre-requisite of the collection of the normal sources of revenue. The best course, therefore, is to remain content for a little longer with an unsound money as a source of revenue, but to introduce immediately a steady unit of account (the relation of which to the unsound money could be officially fixed daily or weekly) as a preliminary to the restoration of the normal sources of revenue.

The recent history of German finance can be summarised thus. Reliance on inflationary taxation, whilst extremely productive to the exchequer in its earliest stages especially whilst the foreign speculator was still buying paper marks, gradually broke down the mark as a serviceable unit of account, one of the effects of which was to render unproductive the greater part of the rest of the revenue-collecting machinery—most taxes being necessarily assessed at some interval of time before they are collected. The failure of the rest of the revenue rendered the Treasury more and more dependent on inflation, until finally the use of legal-tender money had been so far abandoned by the public that even the inflationary tax ceased to be productive and the Government was threatened by literal bankruptcy. At this stage, the fiscal organisation of the country had been so thoroughly destroyed and its social and economic organisation so grievously disordered, as in Russia eighteen months earlier, that it was a perplexing problem to devise ways and means by which the Government could live during the transitional period whilst the normal machinery for collecting revenue was being re-created, especially in face of the struggle with France proceeding at the same time. Nevertheless the problem is not insoluble ; many suggestions could be made ; and a way out will doubtless be found at length.

It is common to speak as though, when a Government pays its way by inflation, the people of the country avoid taxation. We have seen that this is not so. What is raised by printing notes is just as much taken from the public as is a beer-duty or an income-tax. What a Government spends the public pay for. There is no such thing as an uncovered deficit. But in some countries it seems possible to please and content the public, for a time at least, by giving them, in return for the taxes they pay, finely engraved acknowledgements on water-marked paper. The income-tax receipts, which we in England receive from the Surveyor, we throw into the wastepaper basket ; in Germany they call them bank-notes and put them into their pocket-books ; in France they are termed Rentes and are locked up in the family safe.

II. *Currency Depreciation* versus *Capital Levy*

We have seen in the preceding section the extent to which a Government can make use of currency inflation for the purpose of securing income to meet its outgoings. But there is a second way in which inflation helps a Government to make both ends meet, namely by reducing the burden of its pre-existing liabilities in so far as they have been fixed in terms of money. These liabilities consist, in the main, of the internal debt. Every step of depreciation obviously means a reduction in the real claims of the *rentes*-holders against their Government.

It would be too cynical to suppose that, in order to secure the advantages discussed in this section, Governments (except, possibly, the Russian Government) depreciate their currencies *on purpose*. As a rule, they are, or consider themselves to be, driven to it by their necessities. The requirements of the Treasury to meet sudden exceptional outgoings—for a war or to pay the consequences of defeat—are likely to be the original occasion of, at least *temporary*, inflation. But the most cogent reason for *permanent* depreciation, that is to say *Devaluation*, or the policy of fixing the value of the currency permanently at the low level to which a temporary emergency has driven it, is generally to be found in the fact that a restoration of the currency to its former value would raise the recurrent annual

burden of the fixed charges of the National Debt
to an insupportable level.

There is, nevertheless, an alternative to Devaluation
in such cases, provided the opponents of Devaluation
are prepared to face it in time, which they generally
are not,—namely a Capital Levy. The purpose of
this section is to bring out clearly the *alternative*
character of these two methods of moderating the
claims of the *rentier*, when the State's contractual
liabilities, fixed in terms of money, have reached an
excessive proportion of the national income.

The active and working elements in no community,
ancient or modern, will consent to hand over to the
rentier or bond-holding class more than a certain
proportion of the fruits of their work. When the
piled-up debt demands more than a tolerable proportion, relief has usually been sought in one or other
of two out of the three possible methods. The first
is Repudiation. But, except as the accompaniment
of Revolution, this method is too crude, too deliberate,
and too obvious in its incidence. The victims are
immediately aware and cry out too loud ; so that,
in the absence of Revolution, this solution may be
ruled out at present, as regards *internal* debt, in
Western Europe.

The second method is Currency Depreciation,
which becomes Devaluation when it is fixed and
confirmed by law. In the countries of Europe
lately belligerent, this expedient has been adopted

already on a scale which reduces the real burden of the debt by from 50 to 100 per cent. In Germany the National Debt has been by these means practically obliterated, and the bond-holders have lost everything. In France the real burden of the debt is less than a third of what it would be if the franc stood at par ; and in Italy only a quarter. The owners of small savings suffer quietly, as experience shows, these enormous depredations, when they would have thrown down a Government which had taken from them a fraction of the amount by more deliberate but juster instruments.

This fact, however, can scarcely justify such an expedient on its merits. Its indirect evils are many. Instead of dividing the burden between all classes of wealth-owners according to a graduated scale, it throws the whole burden on to the owners of fixed-interest bearing stocks, lets off the *entrepreneur* capitalist and even enriches him, and hits small savings equally with great fortunes. It follows the line of least resistance, and responsibility cannot be brought home to individuals. It is, so to speak, nature's remedy, which comes into silent operation when the body politic has shrunk from curing itself.

The remaining, the scientific, expedient, the Capital Levy, has never yet been tried on a large scale ; and perhaps it never will be. It is the rational, the deliberate method. But it is difficult to explain, and it provokes violent prejudice by coming

into conflict with the deep instincts by which the
love of money protects itself. Unless the patient
understands and approves its purpose, he will not
submit to so severe a surgical operation.

Once Currency Depreciation has done its work, I
should not advocate the unwise, and probably impracticable, policy of retracing the path with the aid of
a Capital Levy.   But if it has become clear that the
claims of the bond-holder are more than the tax-payer
can support, and if there is still time to choose between the policies of a Levy and of further Depreciation, the Levy must surely be preferred on grounds
both of expediency and of justice.   It is an over-
whelming objection to the method of Currency Depreciation, as compared with that of the Levy, that it
falls entirely upon persons whose wealth is in the form
of claims to legal-tender money, and that these are
generally, amongst the capitalists, the poorer capitalists.   It is entirely ungraduated ; it falls on small
savings just as hardly as on big ones ; and incidentally
it benefits the capitalist *entrepreneur* class for the
reasons explained in Chapter I.   Unfortunately the
small savers who have most to lose by Currency
Depreciation are precisely the sort of conservative
people who are most alarmed by a Capital Levy ;
whilst, on the other hand, the *entrepreneur* class
must obviously prefer Depreciation which does not
hit them very much and may actually enrich them.
It is the combination of these two forces which will

generally bring it about that a country will prefer
the inequitable and disastrous courses of Currency
Depreciation to the scientific deliberation of a Levy.

There is a respectable and influential body of
opinion which, repudiating with vehemence the adoption of either expedient, fulminates alike against
Devaluations and Levies, on the ground that they
infringe the untouchable sacredness of contract; or
rather of vested interest, for an alteration of the legal
tender and the imposition of a tax on property are
neither of them in the least illegal or even contrary to
precedent. Yet such persons, by overlooking one of
the greatest of all social principles, namely the fundamental distinction between the right of the individual
to repudiate contract and the right of the State to
control vested interest, are the worst enemies of what
they seek to preserve. For nothing can preserve the
integrity of contract between individuals, except a dis-
cretionary authority in the State to revise what has
become intolerable. The powers of uninterrupted
usury are too great. If the accretions of vested
interest were to grow without mitigation for many
generations, half the population would be no better
than slaves to the other half. Nor can the fact that
in time of war it is easier for the State to borrow than
to tax, be allowed permanently to enslave the taxpayer to the bond-holder. Those who insist that in
these matters the State is in exactly the same position
as the individual, will, if they have their way, render

impossible the continuance of an individualist society, which depends for its existence on moderation.

These conclusions might be deemed obvious if experience did not show that many conservative bankers regard it as more consonant with their cloth, and also as economising thought, to shift public discussion of financial topics off the logical on to an alleged " moral " plane, which means a realm of thought where vested interest can be triumphant over the common good without further debate. But it makes them untrustworthy guides in a perilous age of transition. The State must never neglect the importance of so acting in ordinary matters as to promote certainty and security in business. But when great decisions are to be made, the State is a sovereign body of which the purpose is to promote the greatest good of the whole. When, therefore, we enter the realm of State action, *everything* is to be considered and weighed on its merits. Changes in Death Duties, Income Tax, Land Tenure, Licensing, Game Laws, Church Establishment, Feudal Rights, Slavery, and so on through all ages, have received the same denunciations from the absolutists of contract,—who are the real parents of Revolution.

In our own country the question of the Capital Levy depends for its answer on whether the great increase in the claims of the bond-holder, arising out of the fact that it was easier, and perhaps more expedient, to raise a large part of the current costs of the war by loans rather than by taxes, is more than the taxpayer can be required, in the long run, to support. The high levels of the Death Duties and of the income- and super-taxes on unearned income, by which the net return to the bond-holder is substantially diminished,[1] modify the case. Nevertheless, immediately after the war, when it seemed that the normal budget could scarcely be balanced without a level of taxation of which a tax on earned income at a standard rate between 6s. and 10s. in the £ would be typical, a levy seemed to be necessary. At the present time the case is rather more doubtful. It is not yet possible to know how the normal budget will work out, and much depends on the level at which sterling prices are stabilised. If the level of sterling prices is materially lowered, whether in pursuance of a policy of restoring the old gold parity or for any other reason, a levy may be required. If, however, sterling prices are stabilised somewhere between 80 and 100 per cent above the pre-war level— a settlement probably desirable on other grounds— and if the progressive prosperity of the country is restored, then perhaps we may balance our future budgets without oppressive taxation on earned income and without a levy either. A levy is from the practical view perfectly feasible, and is not open to more objection than any other *new* tax of like magnitude.

---

[1] The net return to the French *rentier* is more than 6 per cent; to the British not much above 3 per cent.

Nevertheless, like all new taxes, it cannot be brought in without friction, and is, therefore, scarcely worth advocating for its own sake merely in substitution for an existing tax of similar incidence. It is to be regarded as the fairest and most expedient method of adjusting the burden of taxation between past accumulations and the fruits of present efforts, whenever, in the general judgment of the country, the discouragement to the latter is excessive. A levy is to be judged, not by itself, but as against the practicable alternatives. Experience shows with great certainty that the active part of the community will not submit in the long run to pay too much to vested interest, and, if the necessary adjustment is not made in one way, it will be made in another,—probably by the depreciation of the currency.

In several countries the existing burden of the internal debt renders Devaluation inevitable and certain sooner or later. It will be sufficient to illustrate the case by reference to the situation of France, —the home of absolutism of all kinds, and hence, sooner or later, of *bouleversement*. The finances of Humpty Dumpty are as follows :

At the end of 1922 the internal debt of France, excluding altogether her external debt, exceeded 250 milliard francs. Further borrowing budgeted for in the ensuing period, together with loans on reconstruction account guaranteed by the Government, may bring this total to the neighbourhood of 300 milliards by the end of 1923. The service of this debt will absorb nearly 18 milliards per annum. The total normal receipts under the provisional[1] Budget for 1923 are estimated at round 23 milliards. That is to say, the service of the debt will shortly absorb, at the value of the franc current early in 1923, almost the entire yield of taxation. Since other Government expenditure in the ordinary budget (*i.e.*, excluding war pensions and future expenditure on reconstruction) cannot be put below 12 milliards a year, it follows that, even on the improbable hypothesis that further expenditure in the extraordinary budget after 1923 will be paid for by Germany, the yield of taxation must be increased permanently by 30 per cent to make both ends meet. If, however, the franc were to depreciate to (say) 100 to the pound sterling, the ordinary budget could be balanced by taking little more of the real income of the country than in 1922.

In these circumstances it will be difficult, if not impossible, to avoid the subtle assistance of a further depreciation. What, then, is to be said of those who still discuss seriously the project of restoring the franc to its former parity ? In such an event the already intolerable burden of the *rentier's* claims

---

[1] The forecasts of the final outcome of the year are frequently changed and may be somewhat different from the above,—though not sufficiently to affect the argument. M. de Lasteyrie has lately pointed out with pride how the further depreciation of the franc, since he first introduced his budget, is already improving the receipts measured in terms of francs.

would be about trebled. It is unthinkable that
the French taxpayer would submit. Even if the
franc were put back to par by a miracle, it could not
stay there. Fresh inflation due to the inadequacy
of tax receipts must drive it anew on its downward
course. Yet I have assumed the cancellation of the
whole of France's external debt, and the assumption
by Germany of the burdens of the extraordinary
budget after 1923, an assumption which is not
justified by present expectations. These facts alone
render it certain that the franc cannot be restored
to its former value.

France must come in due course to some compromise between increasing taxation, and diminishing
expenditure, and reducing what they owe their
rentiers. I have not much doubt that the French
public, as they have hitherto, will consider a further
dose of depreciation—attributing it to the " bad
will " of Germany or to financial Machiavellism in
London and New York—as far more conservative,
orthodox, and in the interest of small savers, than
a justly constructed Capital Levy, the odium of
which could be less easily escaped by the French
Ministry of Finance.

If we look ahead, averting our eyes from the ups
and downs which can make and unmake fortunes in
the meantime, the level of the franc is going to be
settled in the long run not by speculation or the
balance of trade, or even the outcome of the Ruhr

adventure, but by the proportion of his earned income which the French taxpayer will permit to be taken from him to pay the claims of the French *rentier*. The level of the franc exchange will continue to fall until the commodity-value of the francs due to the *rentier* has fallen to a proportion of the national income, which accords with the habits and mentality of the country.

CHAPTER III

THE THEORY OF MONEY AND OF THE
FOREIGN EXCHANGES

THE evil consequences of instability in the standard of value have now been sufficiently described. In this chapter [1] we must lay the theoretical foundations for the practical suggestions of the concluding chapters. Most academic treatises on monetary theory have been based, until lately, on so firm a presumption of a gold standard régime that they need to be adapted to the existing régime of mutually inconvertible paper standards.

I. *The Quantity Theory of Money*

This Theory is fundamental. Its correspondence with fact is not open to question. [2] Nevertheless it is often misstated and misrepresented. Goschen's

---

[1] Parts of this chapter raise, unavoidably, matters of much greater difficulty to the layman than the rest of the book. The reader whose interest in the theoretical foundations is secondary can pass on.

[2] " The Quantity Theory is often defended and opposed as though it were a definite set of propositions that must be either true or false. But in fact the formulæ employed in the exposition of that theory are merely devices for enabling us to bring together in an orderly way the principal causes by which the value of money is determined " (Pigou).

saying of sixty years ago, that "there are many persons who cannot hear the relation of the level of prices to the volume of currency affirmed without a feeling akin to irritation," still holds good.

The Theory flows from the fact that money as such has no utility except what is derived from its exchange-value, that is to say from the utility of the things which it can buy. Valuable articles other than money have a utility in themselves. Provided that they are divisible and transferable, the total amount of this utility increases with their quantity ;—it will not increase in full proportion to the quantity, but, up to the point of satiety, it does increase.

If an article is used for money, such as gold, which has a utility in itself for other purposes, aside from its use as money, the strict statement of the theory, though fundamentally unchanged, is a little complicated. In present circumstances we can excuse ourselves this complication. A Currency Note has no utility in itself and is completely worthless except for the purchasing power which it has as money.

Consequently what the public want is not so many ounces or so many square yards or even so many £ sterling of currency notes, but a quantity sufficient to cover a week's wages, or to pay their bills, or to meet their probable outgoings on a journey or a day's shopping. When people find themselves with more cash than they require for such purposes, they get rid of the surplus by buying goods or investments, or by leaving it for a bank to employ, or, possibly, by increasing their hoarded reserves. Thus the *number* of notes which the public ordinarily have on hand is determined by the amount of *purchasing power* which it suits them to hold or to carry about, and by nothing else. The amount of this purchasing power depends partly on their wealth, partly on their habits. The wealth of the public in the aggregate will only change gradually. Their habits in the use of money —whether their income is paid them weekly or monthly or quarterly, whether they pay cash at shops or run accounts, whether they deposit with banks, whether they cash small cheques at short intervals or larger cheques at longer intervals, whether they keep a reserve or hoard of money about the house—are more easily altered. But if their wealth and their habits in the above respects are unchanged, then the amount of purchasing power which they hold in the form of money is definitely fixed. We can measure this definite amount of purchasing power in terms of a unit made up of a collection of specified quantities of their standard articles of consumption or other objects of expenditure ; for example, the kinds and quantities of articles which are combined for the purpose of a cost-of-living index number. Let us call such a unit a " consumption unit " and assume that the public require to hold an amount of money having a purchasing power over k consumption units. Let there be n currency notes or other forms of cash in circulation with the public, and let p be the price of each consumption unit (*i.e.* p is the index number of the cost of living), then it follows from the above that $n = pk$. This is the famous Quantity Theory of Money. So long as k remains unchanged, n and p rise and fall together; that is to say, the greater or the fewer the number of currency notes, the higher or the lower is the price level in the same proportion.

So far we have assumed that the whole of the public requirement for purchasing power is satisfied by cash, and on the other hand that this requirement is the only source of demand for cash; neglecting the fact that the public, including the business world, employ for the same purpose bank deposits and over-draft facilities, whilst the banks must for the same reason maintain a reserve of cash. The theory is easily extended, however, to cover this case. Let us assume that the public, including the business world, find it convenient to keep the equivalent of k consumption units in cash and of a further k' available at their banks against cheques, and that the banks keep in cash a proportion r of their potential liabilities (k') to the public. Our equation then becomes

$$n = p(k + rk').$$

So long as k, k', and r remain unchanged, we have the same result as before, namely, that n and p rise and fall together. The proportion between k and k'

depends on the banking arrangements of the public ;
the absolute value of these on their habits generally ;
and the value of r on the reserve practices of the banks.
Thus, so long as these are unaltered, we still have a
direct relation between the *quantity* of cash (n) and
the level of prices (p).[1]

We have seen that the amount of k and k' depends
partly on the wealth of the community, partly on its
habits.   Its habits are fixed by its estimation of the
extra convenience of having more cash in hand as
compared with the advantages to be got from spending the cash or investing it.   The point of equilibrium
is reached where the estimated advantages of keeping
more cash in hand compared with those of spending
or investing it about balance.   The matter cannot be
summed up better than in the words of Dr. Marshall :

> In every state of society there is some fraction of their
> income which people find it worth while to keep in the form
> of currency ; it may be a fifth, or a tenth, or a twentieth.   A
> large command of resources in the form of currency renders
> their business easy and smooth, and puts them at an advan-
> tage in bargaining ; but on the other hand it locks up in a
> barren form resources that might yield an income of grati-
> fication if invested, say, in extra furniture ; or a money
> income, if invested in extra machinery or cattle." A man

---

[1] My exposition follows the general lines of Prof. Pigou (*Quarterly
Journal of Economics*, Nov. 1917) and of Dr. Marshall (*Money, Credit, and
Commerce*, I. iv.), rather than the perhaps more familiar analysis of Prof.
Irving Fisher.   Instead of starting with the amount of cash held by the
public, Prof. Fisher begins with the volume of business transacted by means
of money and the frequency with which each unit of money changes hands.
It comes to the same thing in the end and it is easy to pass from the above
formula to Prof. Fisher's ; but the above method of approach seems less
artificial than Prof. Fisher's and nearer to the observed facts.

fixes the appropriate fraction " after balancing one against another the advantages of a further ready command, and the disadvantages of putting more of his resources into a form in which they yield him no direct income or other benefit." " Let us suppose that the inhabitants of a country, taken one with another (and including therefore all varieties of character and of occupation), find it just worth their while to keep by them on the average ready purchasing power to the extent of a tenth part of their annual income, together with a fiftieth part of their property; then the aggregate value of the currency of the country will tend to be equal to the sum of these amounts." [1]

So far there should be no room for difference of opinion. The error often made by careless adherents of the Quantity Theory, which may partly explain why it is not universally accepted, is as follows.

Every one admits that the habits of the public in the use of money and of banking facilities and the practices of the banks in respect of their reserves change from time to time as the result of obvious developments. These habits and practices are a

[1] *Money, Credit, and Commerce*, I. iv. 3. Dr. Marshall shows in a footnote as follows that the above is in fact a development of the traditional way of considering the matter : " Petty thought that the money ' sufficient for ' the nation is ' so much as will pay half a year's rent for all the lands of England and a quarter's rent of the Houseing, for a week's expense of all the people, and about a quarter of the value of all the exported commodities.' Locke estimated that ' one-fiftieth of wages and one-fourth of the landowner's income and one-twentieth part of the broker's yearly returns in ready money will be enough to drive the trade of any country.' Cantillon (A.D. 1755), after a long and subtle study, concludes that the value needed is a ninth of the total produce of the country ; or, what he takes to be the same thing, a third of the rent of the land. Adam Smith has more of the scepticism of the modern age and says : ' it is impossible to determine the proportion,' though ' it has been computed by different authors at a fifth, at a tenth, at a twentieth, and at a thirtieth part of the whole value of the annual produce.' " In modern conditions the normal proportion of the circulation to this national income seems to be somewhere between a tenth and a fifteenth.

reflection of changes in economic and social organisation. But the Theory has often been expounded on
the further assumption that a *mere* change in the
quantity of the currency cannot affect k, r, and k',—
that is to say, in mathematical parlance, that n is an
independent variable in relation to these quantities.
It would follow from this that an arbitrary doubling
of n, since this in itself is assumed not to affect
k, r, and k', must have the effect of raising p to double
what it would have been otherwise. The Quantity
Theory is often stated in this, or a similar, form.

Now " in the long run " this is probably true.
If, after the American Civil War, the American
dollar had been stabilised and defined by law at
10 per cent below its present value, it would be safe
to assume that n and p would now be just 10 per cent
greater than they actually are and that the present
values of k, r, and k' would be entirely unaffected.
But this *long run* is a misleading guide to current
affairs. *In the long run* we are all dead. Economists
set themselves too easy, too useless a task if in
tempestuous seasons they can only tell us that when
the storm is long past the ocean is flat again.

In actual experience, a change of n is liable to
have a reaction both on k and k' and on r. It will
be enough to give a few typical instances. Before
the war (and indeed since) there was a considerable
element of what was conventional and arbitrary in
the reserve policy of the banks, but especially in the

policy of the State Banks towards their gold reserves. These reserves were kept for show rather than for use, and their amount was not the result of close reasoning. There was a decided tendency on the part of these banks between 1900 and 1914 to bottle up gold when it flowed towards them and to part with it reluctantly when the tide was flowing the other way. Consequently, when gold became relatively abundant they tended to hoard what came their way and to raise the proportion of the reserves, with the result that the increased output of South African gold was absorbed with less effect on the price level than would have been the case if an increase of n had been totally without reaction on the value of r.

In agricultural countries where peasants readily hoard money, an inflation, especially in its early stages, does not raise prices proportionately, because when, as a result of a certain rise in the price of agricultural products, more money flows into the pockets of the peasants, it tends to stick there ;—deeming themselves that much richer, the peasants increase the proportion of their receipts that they hoard.

Thus in these and in other ways the terms of our equation tend in their movements to favour the stability of p, and there is a certain friction which prevents a moderate change in n from exercising its full proportionate effect on p.

On the other hand a large change in n, which rubs away the initial friction, and especially a change

in n due to causes which set up a general expectation
of a further change in the same direction, may produce
a *more* than proportionate effect on p. After the
general analysis of Chapter I. and the narratives
of catastrophic inflations given in Chapter II., it is
scarcely necessary to illustrate this further,—it is a
matter more readily understood than it was ten
years ago. A large change in p greatly affects
individual fortunes. Hence a change after it has
occurred, or sooner in so far as it is anticipated, may
greatly affect the monetary habits of the public in
their attempt to protect themselves from a similar
loss in future, or to make gains and avoid loss during
the passage from the equilibrium corresponding to
the old value of n to the equilibrium corresponding
to its new value. Thus after, during, and (so far
as the change is anticipated) before a change in the
value of n, there will be some reaction on the values
of k, k', and r, with the result that the change in the
value of p, at least temporarily and perhaps permanently (since habits and practices, once changed,
will not revert to exactly their old shape), will not be
precisely in proportion to the change in n.

The terms *inflation* and *deflation* are used by
different writers in varying senses. It would be convenient to speak of an increase or decrease in n as
an inflation or deflation of *cash*; and of a decrease
or increase in r as an inflation or deflation of *credit*.
The characteristic of the " credit-cycle " (as the

alternation of boom and depression is now described) consists in a tendency of k and k' to diminish during the boom and increase during the depression, irrespective of changes in n and r, these movements representing respectively a diminution and an increase of " real " balances (*i.e.* balances, in hand or at the bank, measured in terms of purchasing power) ; so that we might call this phenomenon deflation and inflation of real balances.

It will illustrate the " Quantity Theory " equation in . general and the phenomena of deflation and inflation of real balances in particular, if we endeavour to fill in actual values for our symbolic quantities. The following example does not claim to be exact and its object is to illustrate the idea rather than to convey statistically precise facts.   October 1920 was about the end of the recent boom, and October 1922 was near the bottom of the depression.   At these two dates the figures of price level (taking October 1922 as 100), cash circulation (note circulation *plus* private deposits at the Bank of England [1]), and bank deposits in Great Britain were roughly as follows :

	Price Level.	Cash Circulation.	Bank Deposits.
October 1920	150	£585,000,000	£2,000,000,000
October 1922	100	£504,000,000	£1,700,000,000

The value of r was not very different at the two

---

[1] It would take me too far from the immediate matter in hand to discuss why I take this definition of " cash " in the case of Great Britain. It is discussed further in Chapter V. below.

dates—say about 12 per cent. Consequently our equation for the two dates works out as follows[1]:

| October 1920 | $n=585$ | $p=1\cdot5$ | $k=230$ | $k'=1333$ |
| October 1922 | $n=504$ | $p=1$ | $k=300$ | $k'=1700$ |

Thus during the depression k rose from 230 to 300 and k' from 1333 to 1700, which means that the cash holdings of the public at the former date were worth $\frac{23}{30}$, and their bank balances $\frac{1333}{1700}$, of what they were worth at the latter date. It thus appears that the tendency of k and k' to increase had more to do, than the deflation of " cash " had, with the fall of prices between the two periods. If k and k' were to fall back to their 1920 values, prices would rise 30 per cent without any change whatever in the volume of cash or the reserve policy of the banks. Thus even in Great Britain the fluctuations of k and k' can have a decisive influence on the price level ; whilst we have already seen (pp. 51, 52) how enormously they can change in the recent conditions of Russia and Central Europe.

The moral of this discussion, to be carried forward in the reader's mind until we reach Chapters IV. and V., is that the price level is not mysterious, but is governed by a few, definite, analysable influences. Two of these, n and r, are under the direct control (or ought to be) of the central banking authorities. The third, namely k and k', is not directly controllable, and depends on the mood of the public and the business world. The business of stabilising the price level,

---

[1] For $585=1\cdot5(230+1333\times\cdot12)$, and $504=1(300+1700\times\cdot12)$.

not merely over long periods but so as also to avoid
cyclical fluctuations, consists partly in exercising a
stabilising influence over k and k', and, in so far as
this fails or is impracticable, in deliberately varying n
and r so as to *counterbalance* the movement of k and k'.

The usual method of exercising a stabilising influence over k and k', especially over k', is that of
bank-rate. A tendency of k' to increase may be
somewhat counteracted by lowering the bank-rate,
because easy lending diminishes the advantage of
keeping a margin for contingencies in cash. Cheap
money also operates to *counterbalance* an increase of
k', because, by encouraging borrowing from the banks,
it prevents r from increasing or causes r to diminish.
But it is doubtful whether bank-rate by itself is
always a powerful enough instrument, and, if we are
to achieve stability, we must be prepared to vary n
and r on occasion.

Our analysis suggests that the first duty of the
central banking and currency authorities is to make
sure that they have n and r thoroughly under control.
For example, so long as inflationary taxation is in
question n will be influenced by other than currency
objects and cannot, therefore, be fully under control ;
moreover, at the other extreme, under a gold standard
n is not always under control, because it depends on
the unregulated forces which determine the demand
and supply of gold throughout the world. Again,
without a central banking system r will not be under

proper control because it will be determined by the unco-ordinated decisions of numerous different banks.

At the present time in Great Britain r is very completely controlled, and n also, so long as we refrain from inflationary finance on the one hand and from a return to an unregulated gold standard on the other.[1] The second duty of the authorities is therefore worth discussing, namely, the *use* of their control over n and r to counterbalance changes in k and k'. Even if k and k' were entirely outside the influence of deliberate policy, which is not in fact the case, nevertheless p could be kept reasonably steady by suitable modifications of the values of n and r.

Old-fashioned advocates of sound money have laid too much emphasis on the need of keeping n and r steady, and have argued as if this policy by itself would produce the right results. So far from this being so, steadiness of n and r, when k and k' are not steady, is bound to lead to unsteadiness of the price level. Cyclical fluctuations are characterised, not primarily by changes in n or r, but by changes in k and k'. It follows that they can only be cured if we are ready deliberately to increase and decrease n and r, when symptoms of movement are showing in the values of k and k'. I am being led, however, into a large subject beyond my immediate purpose, and am anticipating also the topic of Chapter V.

[1] In the case of the United States the same thing is more or less true, so long as the Federal Reserve Board is prepared to incur the expense of bottling up redundant gold.

These hints will serve, nevertheless, to indicate to the reader what a long way we may be led by an understanding of the implications of the simple Quantity equation with which we started.

II. *The Theory of Purchasing Power Parity.*

The Quantity Theory deals with the purchasing power or commodity-value of a given national currency. We come now to the *relative* value of *two* distinct national currencies,—that is to say, to the theory of the Foreign Exchanges.

When the currencies of the world were nearly all on a gold basis, their relative value (*i.e.* the exchanges) depended on the actual amount of gold metal in a unit of each, with minor adjustments for the cost of transferring the metal from place to place.

When this common measure has ceased to be effective and we have instead a number of independent systems of inconvertible paper, what basic fact determines the rates at which units of the different currencies exchange for one another ?

The explanation is to be found in the doctrine, as old in itself as Ricardo, with which Professor Cassel has lately familiarised the public under the name of " Purchasing Power Parity." [1]

[1] This term was first introduced into economic literature in an article contributed by Prof. Cassel to the *Economic Journal*, December 1918. For Prof. Cassel's considered opinions on the whole question, see his *Money and Foreign Exchange after 1914* (1922). The theory, as distinct from the name, is essentially Ricardo's.

This doctrine in its baldest form runs as follows : (1) The purchasing power of an inconvertible currency within its own country, *i.e.* the currency's *internal* purchasing power, depends on the currency policy of the Government and the currency habits of the people, in accordance with the Quantity Theory of Money just discussed. (2) The purchasing power of an inconvertible currency in a foreign country, *i.e.* the currency's *external* purchasing power, must be the rate of exchange between the home-currency and the foreign-currency, multiplied by the foreign-currency's purchasing power in its own country. (3) In conditions of equilibrium the *internal* and *external* purchasing powers of a currency must be the *same*, allowance being made for transport charges and import and export taxes ; for otherwise a movement of trade would occur in order to take advantage of the inequality. (4) It follows, therefore, from (1), (2), and (3) that the rate of exchange between the home-currency and the foreign-currency must tend in equilibrium to be the ratio between the purchasing powers of the home-currency at home and of the foreign-currency in the foreign country. This ratio between the respective home purchasing powers of the two currencies is designated their " purchasing power parity."

If, therefore, we find that the internal and external purchasing powers of the home-currency are widely different, and, which is the same thing, that the actual exchange rates differ widely from the purchas-

ing power parities, then we are justified in inferring
that equilibrium is not established, and that, as time
goes on, forces will come into play to bring the actual
exchange rates and the purchasing power parities
nearer together. The actual exchanges are often
more sensitive and more volatile than the purchasing
power parities, being subject to speculation, to sudden
movements of funds, to seasonal influences, and to
anticipations of impending changes in purchasing
power parity (due to relative inflation or deflation);
though also on other occasions they may lag behind.
Nevertheless it is the purchasing power parity,
according to this doctrine, which corresponds to the
old gold par. This is the point about which the
exchanges fluctuate, and at which they must ultimately come to rest; with one material difference,
namely, that it is not itself a fixed point,—since, if
internal prices move differently in the two countries
under comparison, the purchasing power parity also
moves, so that equilibrium may be restored, not only
by a movement in the market rate of exchange, but also
by a movement of the purchasing power parity itself.

At first sight this theory appears to be one of great
practical utility; and many persons have endeavoured
to draw important practical conclusions about the
future course of the exchanges from charts exhibiting
the divergences between the market rate of exchange
and the purchasing power parities,—undeterred by
the perplexity whether an existing divergence from

equilibrium will be remedied by a movement of the exchanges or of the purchasing power parity or of both.

In practical applications of the doctrine there are, however, two further difficulties, which we have allowed so far to escape our attention,—both of them arising out of the words *allowance being made for transport charges and import and export taxes*. The first difficulty is how to make allowance for such charges and taxes. The second difficulty is how to treat purchasing power over goods and services which *do not enter into international trade at all*.

The doctrine, in the form in which it is generally applied, endeavours to deal with the first difficulty by assuming that the percentage difference between internal and external purchasing power at some standard date, when approximate equilibrium may be presumed to have existed, generally the year 1913, may be taken as an approximately satisfactory correction for the same disturbing factors at the present time. For example, instead of calculating directly the cost of a standard set of goods at home and abroad respectively, the calculations are made that $2 are required to buy in the United States a standard set which $1 would have bought in 1913, and that £2·43 are required to buy in England what £1 would have bought in 1913. On this basis (the pre-war purchasing power parity being assumed to be in equilibrium with the pre-war exchange of $4·86 = £1) the present purchasing power parity between dollars and sterling is given by $4 = £1, since $4 \cdot 86 \times 2 \div 2 \cdot 43 = 4$.

The obvious objection to this method of correction is that transport and tariff costs, especially if this term is taken to cover all export and import regulations, including prohibitions and official or semi-official combines for differentiating between export and home prices, are notoriously widely different in many cases from those which existed in 1913. We should not get the same result if we were to take some year other than 1913 as the basis of the calculation.

The second difficulty—the treatment of purchasing power over articles which do not enter into international trade—is still more serious. For, if we restrict ourselves to articles entering into international trade and make exact allowance for transport and tariff costs, we should find that the theory is always in accordance with the facts, with perhaps a short time-lag, the purchasing power parity being never very far from the market rate of exchange. Indeed, it is the whole business of the international merchant to see that this is so ; for whenever the rates are temporarily out of parity he is in a position to make a profit by moving goods. The prices of cotton in New York, Liverpool, Havre, Hamburg, Genoa, and Prague, expressed in dollars, sterling, francs, marks, lire, and krone respectively, are never for any length of time much divergent from one another on the

basis of the exchange rates actually obtaining in the
market, due allowance being made for tariffs and the
cost of moving cotton from one centre to another ;
and the same is true of other articles of international
trade, though with an increasing time-lag as we pass
to articles which are not standardised or are not
handled in organised markets. In fact, the theory,
stated thus, is a truism, and as nearly as possible
jejune.

For this reason practical applications of the theory
are not thus restricted. The standard set of commodities selected is not confined to goods which are
exported from and imported into the countries under
comparison, but is the same set, generally speaking,
as is used for compiling index numbers of general
purchasing power or of the working-class cost of
living. Yet applied in this way—namely, in a comparison of movements of the *general* index numbers
of home prices in two countries with movements
in the rates of exchange between their currencies
—the theory requires a further assumption for its
validity, namely, that in the long run the home
prices of the goods and services which do not enter
into international trade, move in more or less the
same proportions as those which do.[1]

---

[1] " Our calculation of the purchasing power parity rests strictly on the
proviso that the rise in prices in the countries concerned has affected all
commodities in a like degree. If that proviso is not fulfilled, then the actual
exchange rate may deviate from the calculated purchasing power parity."
Cassel, *Money and Foreign Exchange after 1914*, p. 154.

So far from this being a truism, it is not literally or exactly true at all ; and one can only say that it is more or less true according to circumstances.   If capital and labour can freely move on a large scale between home and export industries without loss of relative efficiency, if there is no movement in the " equation of exchange " (see below) with the other country, and if the fluctuations in price are solely due to monetary influences and not to changes in other economic relationships between the two countries, then this further assumption may be approximately justified.   But this is not always the case ; and such a cataclysm as the war, with its various consequences to victor and vanquished, may set up a new equilibrium position.   There may, for example, be a change more or less permanent, or at least as prolonged as the reparation payments, in the relative exchange values of Germany's imports and exports respectively, or of those German products and services which can enter into international trade and those which cannot.   Or, again, the strengthening of the financial position of the United States as against Europe, which has resulted from the war, may have shifted the old equilibrium in a direction favourable to the United States.   In such cases it is not correct to assume that the coefficients of purchasing power parity, calculated, as they generally are calculated, by means of the relative variations of index numbers of general purchasing power from their pre - war levels, must ultimately approximate to the actual rates of exchange, or that internal and external purchasing power must ultimately bear to one another the same relation as in 1913.

The Index Number calculated for the United States by the Federal Reserve Board illustrates how disturbing may be the influence of the change since 1913 in the relative prices of imported goods, exported goods, and commodities generally :

	Goods Imported.	Goods Exported.	All Commodities.
1913	100	100	100
July 1922 . . .	128	165	165
April 1923 . . .	156	186	169
July 1923 . . .	141	170	159

Thus the theory does not provide a simple or ready-made measure of the "true" value of the exchanges. When it is restricted to foreign-trade goods, it is little better than a truism. When it is not so restricted, the conception of purchasing power parity becomes much more interesting, but is no longer an accurate forecaster of the course of the foreign exchanges. If, therefore, we follow the ordinary practice of fixing purchasing power parity by comparisons of the *general* purchasing power of a country's currency at home and abroad, then we must not infer from this that the actual rate of exchange *ought* to stand at the purchasing power parity, or that it is only a matter of time and adjustment before the two will return to equality. Purchasing power parity, thus defined, tells us an important fact about the relative changes in the purchasing power of money in (*e.g.*) England and the United States or Germany between 1913 and, say, 1923, but it does not necessarily settle what the equilibrium exchange rate in 1923 between sterling and dollars or marks ought to be.

Thus defined " purchasing power parity " deserves attention, even though it is not always an accurate forecaster of the foreign exchanges. The practical importance of our qualifications must not be exaggerated. If the fluctuations of purchasing power parity are markedly different from the fluctuations in the exchanges, this indicates an actual or impending change in the relative prices of the two classes of goods which respectively do and do not enter into international trade. Now there is certainly a tendency for movements in the prices of these two classes of goods to influence one another in the long run. The relative valuation placed on them is derived from deep economic and psychological causes which are not easily disturbed. If, therefore, the divergence from the pre-existing equilibrium is mainly due to monetary causes (as, for example, different degrees of inflation or deflation in the two countries), as it often is, then we may reasonably expect that purchasing power parity and exchange value will come together again before long.

When this is the case, it is not possible to say

in general whether exchange value will move towards purchasing power parity or the other way
round. Sometimes, as recently in Europe, it is the
exchanges which are the more sensitive to impending
relative price-changes and move first; whilst in
other cases the exchanges may not move until after
the change in the relation between the internal
and external price-levels is an accomplished fact.
But the essence of the purchasing power parity
theory, considered as an explanation of the exchanges, is to be found, I think, in its regarding
internal purchasing power as being in the long run
a more trustworthy indicator of a currency's value
than the market rates of exchange, because internal
purchasing power quickly reflects the monetary policy
of the country, which is the final determinant. If the
market rates of exchange fall further than the country's
existing or impending currency policy justifies by its
effect on the internal purchasing power of the country's
money, then sooner or later the exchange value is
bound to recover. Thus, provided no persisting
change is taking place in the basic economic relations
between two countries, and provided the internal
purchasing power of the currency has in each country
settled down to equilibrium in relation to the currency
policy of the authorities, then the rate of exchange
between the currencies of the two countries must also
settle down in the long run to correspond with their
comparative internal purchasing powers. Subject to

these assumptions comparative internal purchasing power does take the place of the old gold parity as furnishing the point about which the short-period movements of the exchanges fluctuate.

If, on the other hand, these assumptions are not fulfilled and changes are taking place in the "equation of exchange," as economists call it, between the services and products of one country and those of another, either on account of movements of capital, or reparation payments, or changes in the relative efficiency of labour, or changes in the urgency of the world's demand for that country's special products, or the like, then the equilibrium point between purchasing power parity and the rate of exchange may be modified permanently.

This point may be made clearer by an example. Let us consider two countries, Westropa and the United States of the Hesperides, and let us assume for the sake of simplicity, and also because it may often correspond to the facts, that in both countries the price of exported goods moves in the same way as the price of other home-produced goods, but that the "equation of exchange" has moved in favour of the Hesperides so that a smaller number than before of units of Hesperidean products exchange for a given quantity of Westropean products. It follows from this that imported products in Westropa will rise in price more than commodities generally, whilst in the Hesperides they will rise less. Let us suppose

that between 1913 and 1923 the Westropean index
number of prices has risen from 100 to 155 and the
Hesperidean index number from 100 to 160 ; that
these index numbers are so constructed in each case
that imported commodities constitute 20 per cent
and home-produced commodities 80 per cent of the
whole ; and that the " equation of exchange " has
moved 10 per cent in favour of the Hesperides, that
is to say a given quantity of the goods exported by
the Hesperides will buy 10 per cent more than before
of the goods exported by Europe.   The state of affairs
is then as follows : [1]

Westropa :	Price index of imported commodities	(x)	167.
	,,	home-produced ,,	(y)	152.
	,,	all ,,		155.
Hesperides :	,,	imported ,,	(x')	148.
	,,	home-produced ,,	(y')	163.
	,,	all ,,		160.

Thus it appears that the purchasing power parity of
the Westropean currency in 1923 compared with 1913
is $\left(\dfrac{160}{155}=\right)103$; whereas the rate of exchange, compared with the 1913 parity, is $\left(\dfrac{163}{167}=\dfrac{148}{152}=\right)97$.   If
the worsening of Westropa's equation of exchange
with the Hesperides is permanent, then its purchasing
power parity (on the 1913 basis) will also remain
permanently above the equilibrium value of the
market rate of exchange.

[1] For $10x=11y$ $11x'=10y'$
$8y+2x=1550$ $8y'+2x'=1600.$

A tendency of these two measures of the value of a country's currency to move differently is, therefore, a highly interesting symptom. If the market rate of exchange shows a continuing tendency to stand below the purchasing power parity, we have, failing any other explanation, some reason to suspect a worsening of the " equation of exchange " as compared with the base year.

In the charts and tables below, the actual results are worked out of applying the theory to the exchange value of sterling, francs, and lire in terms of dollars since 1919. The figures show that, quantitatively speaking, the influences, which detract from the precision of the purchasing power parity theory, have been in these cases small, on the whole, as compared with those which function in accord with it. There seems to have been some disturbance in the " equations of exchange " since 1913,—which would probably show up more distinctly if it were not that the index numbers employed in the following enquiry are of the type which is largely built up from articles entering into international trade. Nevertheless general price changes, affecting all commodities more or less equally, due to currency inflation or deflation, have been so dominant in their influence that the theory has been actually applicable with remarkable accuracy. In the case, however, of such countries as Germany, where the shocks to equilibrium have been much more violent in many respects, the concordance between the purchasing power parity based on 1913 and the actual rate of exchange has suffered, whether temporarily or permanently, very great disturbance.

The first of these charts, which deals with the value of sterling in terms of dollars, shows that whilst the purchasing power parity, calculated with 1913 as base, is often somewhat above the actual exchange, there is a persevering tendency for the two to come together. The two curves are within one point of each other in September-November 1919, March - April 1920, April 1921, September 1921, January-June 1922, and February-June 1923, which is certainly a remarkable illustration of the tendency to concordance between the purchasing power parity and the rate of exchange. On inductive grounds it would be tempting to conclude from this chart that the financial consequences of the war have depressed the equilibrium of the purchasing power parity of sterling as against the dollar from 1 to $2\frac{1}{2}$ per cent since 1913, if it were not that this figure barely exceeds the margin of error resulting from the choice of one pair of index numbers rather than another from amongst those available.[1] It will be interesting to see what effect is produced by the payment, just commenced, of the interest on the American debt.

This chart brings out clearly, as also do those for

[1] Nevertheless, if I had used the Board of Trade or the *Statist* index number in place of the *Economist* index number in the table below, the presumption of a slight worsening of the " equation of index " against Great Britain would be somewhat strengthened.

France and Italy, the susceptibility of the foreign exchange rates to seasonal influences, whereas the purchasing power parity is naturally less affected by them.

In the case of France the curves are together at the end of 1919, diverge in 1920, come together again in the middle of 1921, and keep together until a divergence occurred again in the latter part of 1922.

For Italy, rather unexpectedly perhaps, the relationship is extraordinarily steady, although here, as in the case of France and Great Britain, there are indications that the war may have resulted in a slight lowering of the equilibrium point, by (say) 10 per cent ; [1]—the parity, calculated with 1913 as the base year, has been almost invariably somewhat above the actual rate of exchange. The Italian curve illustrates in a remarkable way the manner in which the external and internal purchasing powers of the currency fall together, when the main influence at work is a progressive depreciation due to currency inflation.

The broad effect of these curves and tables is to give substantial inductive support to the general theory outlined above, even under such abnormal conditions as have existed since the Armistice. During this period the movements of the relative price level in France and Italy due to monetary inflation have been

[1] The use of any of the other Italian index numbers would have accentuated this indication. The table of American prices given on p. 94 above confirms the suggestion that the " equation of exchange " between the U.S. and the rest of the world as a whole has moved, say, 10 per cent in favour of the former.

GREAT BRITAIN AND THE UNITED STATES

Per cent of 1913 Parity.	Price Index Number.		Purchasing Power Parity.[3]	Actual Exchange (Monthly Average).
	Great Britain.[1]	United States.[2]		
1919 Aug. .	242	216	89·3	87·6
Sept. .	245	210	85·7	85·8
Oct. .	252	211	83·7	85·9
Nov. .	259	217	83·8	84·3
Dec. .	273	223	81·7	78·4
1920 Jan. .	289	233	81·0	75·6
Feb. .	303	232	76·6	69·5
March .	310	234	75·6	76·2
April .	306	245	80·1	80·6
May .	305	247	81·0	79·0
June .	291	243	83·5	81·1
July .	293	241	82·3	79·4
Aug. .	288	231	80·2	74·2
Sept. .	284	226	79·6	72·2
Oct. .	266	211	79·3	71·4
Nov. .	246	196	79·7	70·7
Dec. .	220	179	81·4	71·4
1921 Jan. .	209	170	81·4	76·7
Feb. .	192	160	83·3	79·6
March .	189	155	82·0	80·3
April .	183	148	80·9	80·7
May .	182	145	79·7	81·5
June .	179	142	79·3	78·0
July .	178	141	79·2	74·8
Aug. .	179	142	79·3	75·1
Sept. .	183	141	77·0	76·5
Oct. .	170	142	83·5	79·5
Nov. .	166	141	84·9	81·5
Dec. .	162	140	86·4	85·3
1922 Jan. .	159	138	86·8	86·8
Feb. .	158	141	89·1	89·6
March .	160	142	88·7	89·9
April .	159	143	89·9	90·7
May .	162	148	91·4	91·4
June .	163	150	92·0	91·5
July .	163	155	95·1	91·4
Aug. .	158	155	98·1	91·7
Sept. .	156	153	98·1	91·1
Oct. .	158	154	97·4	91·2
Nov. .	159	156	98·1	92·0
Dec. .	158	156	98·7	94·6
1923 Jan. .	160	156	97·5	95·7
Feb. .	163	157	96·3	96·2
March .	163	159	97·5	96·5
April .	165	159	96·4	95·7
May .	164	156	95·1	95·0
June .	160	153	95·6	94·8

[1] *Economist* Index Number.   [2] U.S. Bureau of Labour Index Number, as revised.
[3] The U.S. Bureau of Labour Index Number divided by the *Economist* Index Number.

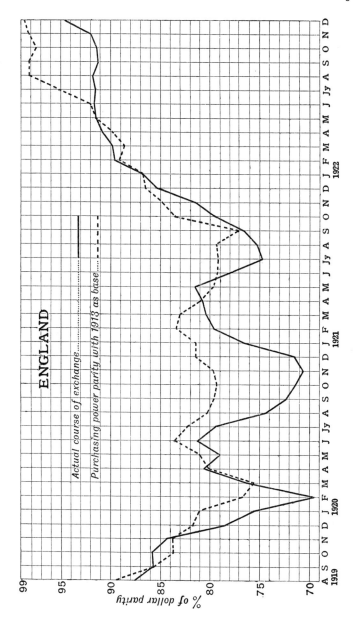

ENGLAND

Actual course of exchange.........................

Purchasing power parity with 1913 as base........

Per cent of 1913 Parity.	Purchasing Power Parity.[1]	Actual Exchange.	Per cent of 1913 Parity.	Purchasing Power Parity.[1]	Actual Exchange.
1919 Aug. .	62	66	1921 Aug. .	43	40
Sept. .	58	61	Sept. .	41	38
Oct. .	55	60	Oct. .	43	38
Nov. .	53	55	Nov. .	42	37
Dec. .	52	48	Dec. .	43	40
1920 Jan. .	48	44	1922 Jan. .	44	42
Feb. .	44	36	Feb. .	46	45
March .	42	37	March .	46	47
April .	41	32	April .	46	48
May .	45	35	May .	44	47
June .	49	41	June .	46	45
July .	48	42	July .	48	43
Aug. .	46	37	Aug. .	47	41
Sept. .	43	35	Sept. .	46	40
Oct. .	42	34	Oct. .	46	38
Nov. .	43	31	Nov. .	44	35
Dec. .	41	30	Dec. .	43	37
1921 Jan. .	42	33	1923 Jan. .	40	34
Feb. .	42	37	Feb. .	37	32
March .	43	36	March .	37	33
April .	43	37	April .	38	35
May .	44	43	May .	38	34
June .	44	42	June .	37	33
July .	43	40			

[1] U.S. Bureau of Labour Index divided by French official wholesale Index.

ITALY AND THE UNITED STATES

Per cent of 1913 Parity.	Purchasing Power Parity.[1]	Actual Exchange.	Per cent of 1913 Parity.	Purchasing Power Parity.[1]	Actual Exchange.
1919 Aug. .	59	56	1921 Aug. .	26	22
Sept. .	56	53	Sept. .	24	22
Oct. .	54	51	Oct. .	24	20
Nov. .	50	44	Nov. .	24	21
Dec. .	49	40	Dec. .	23	23
1920 Jan. .	46	37	1922 Jan. .	24	23
Feb. .	42	29	Feb. .	25	25
March .	38	28	March .	27	26
April .	36	23	April .	27	28
May .	38	27	May .	28	27
June .	40	31	June .	28	26
July .	39	30	July .	28	24
Aug. .	37	25	Aug. .	27	23
Sept. .	34	23	Sept. .	26	22
Oct. .	32	20	Oct. .	26	22
Nov. .	30	19	Nov. .	26	23
Dec. .	28	18	Dec. .	27	26
1921 Jan. .	26	18	1923 Jan. .	27	26
Feb. .	26	19	Feb. .	27	25
March .	26	20	March .	27	25
April .	25	24	April .	27	26
May .	27	27	May .	27	25
June .	28	26	June .	26	24
July .	27	24			

[1] U.S. Bureau of Labour Index Number divided by the " Bachi " Index Number.

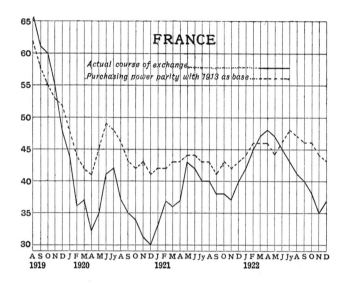

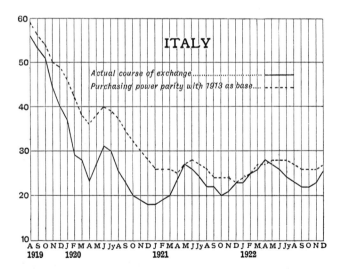

so much larger than any shifting in the " equation of exchange " (a movement of more than 10 or 20 per cent in which would be startling) that their foreign exchanges have been much more influenced by their internal price policy in relation to the internal price policies of other countries than by any other factor ; with the result that the Purchasing Power Parity Theory, even in its crude form, has worked passably well.

III. *The Seasonal Fluctuation.*

Thus the Theory of Purchasing Power Parity tells us that movements in the rate of exchange between the currencies of two countries tend, subject to adjustment in respect of movements in the " equation of exchange," to correspond pretty closely to movements in the internal price levels of the two countries each expressed in their own currency.   It follows that the rate of exchange can be improved in favour of one of the countries by a financial policy directed towards a lowering of its internal price level relatively to the internal price level of the other country.   On the other hand a financial policy which has the effect of raising the internal price level must result, sooner or later, in depressing the rate of exchange.

The conclusion is generally drawn, and quite correctly, that budgetary deficits covered by a progressive inflation of the currency render the stabilisation of a country's exchanges impossible ; and that

III   *THEORY OF MONEY AND THE EXCHANGES*   107

the cessation of any increase in the volume of currency, due to this cause, is a necessary pre-requisite to a successful attempt at stabilising.

The argument, however, is often carried further than this, and it is supposed that, if a country's budget, currency, foreign trade, and its internal and external price levels are properly adjusted, then, automatically, its foreign exchange will be steady.[1] So long, therefore, as the exchanges fluctuate—thus the argument runs—this in itself is a symptom that an attempt to stabilise would be premature. When, on the other hand, the basic conditions necessary for stabilisation are present, the exchange will steady itself. In short, any deliberate or artificial scheme of stabilisation is attacking the problem at the wrong end. It is the regulation of the currency, by means of sound budgetary and bank-rate policies, that needs attention. The proclamation of convertibility will be the last and crowning stage of the proceedings, and will amount to little more than the announcement of a *fait accompli*.

There is a certain force in this mode of reasoning. But in one important respect it is fallacious.

Even though foreign trade is properly adjusted, and the country's claims and liabilities on foreign

---

[1] Dr. R. Estcourt, criticising one of my articles in *The Annalist* for June 12, 1922, writes : " The arrangement would not last for any appreciable period unless, as a preliminary, the Governments took the necessary steps to balance their budgets. If that were done, the so-called stabilisation speedily would become unnecessary ; exchange would stabilise itself at pre-war rates." This passage puts boldly an opinion which is widely held.

account are in equilibrium over the year as a whole, it does not follow that they are in equilibrium every day. Indeed, it is well known that countries which import large quantities of agricultural produce do not find it convenient, if they are to secure just the quality and the amount which they require, to buy at an equal rate throughout the year, but prefer to concentrate their purchases on the autumn period.[1] Thus, quite consistently with equilibrium over the year as a whole, industrial countries tend to owe money to agricultural countries in the second half of the year, and to repay in the first half. The satisfaction of these seasonal requirements for credit with the least possible disturbance to trade was recognised

---

[1] Whilst the fact of seasonal pressure is well ascertained, the exact analysis of it is a little complicated. Food arrivals into Great Britain, for example, are nearly 10 per cent heavier in the third and fourth quarters of the year than in the first and second, and reach their maximum in the fourth quarter. (These and the following figures are based on averages for the pre-war period 1901–1913 worked out by the Cambridge and London Economic Service). Raw material imports are more than 20 per cent heavier in the fourth and first quarters than in the second and third, and reach their maximum in the three months November to January. Thus the fourth quarter of the year is the period at which there are heavy imports of both food and raw materials. Manufactured exports, on the other hand, are distributed through the year much more evenly, and are about normal during the last quarter. Allowing for the fact that imports are paid for, generally speaking, before they arrive, these dates correspond pretty closely with the date at which seasonal pressure is actually experienced by the dollar-sterling exchange. In France, since the war, imports in the last quarter of the year seem to have been quite 50 per cent heavier than, for example, in the first quarter. In Italy the third quarter seems to be the slackest, and the last quarter, again, a relatively heavy period. When we turn to the statistics for the United States we find the other side of the picture. August and September are the months of heavy wheat export ; October to January those of heavy cotton export. The strength of the dollar exchanges in the early autumn is further increased by the financial pressure in the United States during the crop-moving period, which leads to a withdrawal of funds from foreign centres to New York.

before the war as an important function of international banking, and the seasonal transference of
short-term credits from one centre to another was
carried out for a moderate commission.

It was possible for this service to be rendered
cheaply because, with the certainty provided by
convertibility, the price paid for it did not need to
include any appreciable provision against risk. A
somewhat higher rate of discount in the temporarily
debtor country, together with a small exchange
profit provided by the slight shift of the exchanges
within the gold points, was quite sufficient.

But what is the position now ? As always, the
balance of payments must balance every day. As
before, the balance of trade is spread unevenly
through the year. Formerly the daily balance was
adjusted by the movement of bankers' funds, as
described above. But now it is no longer a purely
bankers' business, suitably and sufficiently rewarded
by an arbitrage profit. If a banker moves credits
temporarily from one country to another, he cannot
be certain at what rate of exchange he will be able
to bring them back again later on. Even though
he may have a strong opinion as to the probable
course of exchange, his profit is no longer definitely
calculable beforehand, as it used to be ; he has learnt
by experience that unforeseen movements of the
exchange may involve him in heavy loss ; and his
prospective profit must be commensurate with the

risk he runs. Even if he thinks that the risk is covered actuarially by the prospective profit, a banker cannot afford to run such risks on a large scale. In fact, the seasonal adjustment of credit requirements has ceased to be arbitrage banking business, and demands the services of speculative finance.

Under present conditions, therefore, a large fluctuation of the exchange may be necessary before the daily account can be balanced, even though the annual account is level. Where in the old days a banker would have readily remitted millions to and from New York, hundreds of thousands are now as much as the biggest institutions will risk. The exchange must fall (or rise, as the case may be) until either the speculative financier feels sufficiently confident of a large profit to step in, or the merchant, appalled by the rate of exchange quoted to him for the transaction, decides to forgo the convenience of purchasing at that particular season of the year, and postpones a part of his purchases.

The services of the professional exchange speculator, being discouraged by official and banking influences, are generally in short supply, so that a heavy price has to be paid for them, and trade is handicapped by a corresponding expense, in so far as it continues to purchase its materials at the most convenient season of the year.

The extent to which the exchange fluctuations which have troubled trade during the past three years have been seasonal, and therefore due, not to a continuing or increasing disequilibrium, but *merely* to the absence of a fixed exchange, is not, I think, fully appreciated.

During 1919 there was a heavy fall of the chief European exchanges due to the termination of the inter-Allied arrangements which had existed during the war. During 1922 there was a rise of the sterling exchange, which was independent of seasonal influences. During 1923 there has been a further non-seasonal collapse of the franc exchange due to certain persisting features of France's internal finances and external policy. But the following table shows how largely *recurrent* the fluctuations have been during the four years since the autumn of 1919 :—

PERCENTAGE OF DOLLAR PARITY

August-July.	Sterling.		Francs.		Lire.	
	Lowest.	Highest.	Lowest.	Highest.	Lowest.	Highest.
1919–1920	69	88	31	66	22	56
1920–1921	69	82	30	45	18	29
1921–1922	73	92	37	48	20	28
1922–1923	90	97	29	41	20	27

On the experience of the past three years, francs and lire are at their best in April and May and at their worst between October and December. Sterling is not quite so punctual in its movements, the best point of the year falling somewhere between March and June and the worst between August and November.

The comparative stability of the highest and lowest quotations respectively in each year, especially in the case of Italy, is very striking, and indicates that a policy of stabilisation at some mean figure might have been practicable ; whilst, on the other hand, the wide divergences between the highest and lowest are a measure of the expense and interference that trade has suffered.

These results correspond so closely to the facts of seasonal trade (see above, p. 108) that we may safely attribute most of the major fluctuations of the exchanges from month to month to the actual pressure of trade remittances, and not to speculation.   Speculators, indeed, by anticipating the movements tend to make them occur a little earlier than they would occur otherwise, but by thus spreading the pressure more evenly through the year their influence is to diminish the absolute amount of the fluctuation. General opinion greatly overestimates the influence of exchange-speculators acting under the stimulus of merely political and sentimental considerations. Except for brief periods the influence of the speculator is washed out ; and political events can only exert a lasting influence on the exchanges, in so far as they modify the internal price level, the volume of trade, or the ability of a country to borrow on foreign markets. A political event, which does not materially affect any of these facts, cannot exert a lasting effect on the exchanges merely by its influence on sentiment. The only important exception to this statement is where there exists on a large scale a long-period speculative investment in a country's currency on the part of foreigners, as in the case of German marks. But such investments are comparable to borrowing abroad and exercise a different kind of influence altogether from a speculative transaction proper, which is opened with the intention of its being closed again within a short period. And even speculative investment in a currency, since it is bound to diminish sooner or later, cannot permanently prevent the exchanges from reaching the equilibrium justified by conditions of trading and relative price levels.

It follows that, whilst purely seasonal fluctuations do not interfere with the forces which determine the ultimate equilibrium of the exchanges, nevertheless stability of the exchange from day to day cannot be maintained merely by the *fact* of stability in these underlying conditions. It is necessary also that bankers should have a sufficiently certain *expectation* of such stability to induce them to look after the daily and seasonal fluctuations of the market in return for a moderate commission.

After recent experience it is unlikely that they will actually entertain any such expectation, even if the underlying facts were of a kind to justify it, with sufficient conviction to act, unless it is backed up by a guarantee on the part of the Central Authority

(Bank or Government) to employ all their resources for the maintenance of the level of exchange at a stated figure. At present the declared official policy is to bring the franc and the lira (for example) back to par, so that operations favouring a fall of these currencies are not free from danger. On the other hand no steps are taken to make this policy effective, and the conditions of internal finance in France and Italy indicate that their exchanges may go much worse. Thus, since no one can have complete confidence whether they are to be a great deal better or very much worse, there must be a wide fluctuation before financiers will come in, purely from motives of self-interest, to balance the day-to-day fluctuations and the month-to-month fluctuations round about the unpredictable point of equilibrium.

If, therefore, the exchanges are not stabilised by policy, they will never come to an equilibrium of themselves. As time goes on and experience accumulates, the oscillations may be smaller than at present. Speculators may come in a little sooner, and importers may make greater efforts to spread their requirements more evenly over the year. But even so, there must be a substantial difference of rates between the busy season and the slack season, until the business world knows for certain at what level the exchanges in question are going to settle down. Thus a seasonal fluctuation of the exchanges (including the sterling-dollar exchange) is inevitable, even in the absence of any decided long-period tendency of an exchange to rise or to fall, unless the Central Authority, by a guarantee of convertibility or otherwise, takes special steps to provide against it.

IV. *The Forward Market in Exchanges.*

When a merchant buys or sells goods in a foreign currency the transaction is not always for immediate settlement by cash or negotiable bill. During the interval before he can cover himself by buying or selling (as the case may be) the foreign currency involved, he runs an exchange risk, losses or gains on which may often, in these days, swamp his trading profit. He is thus involuntarily engaged in a heavy risk of a kind which it is hardly in his province to undertake. The subject of what follows is a piece of financial machinery—namely, the market in " forward " exchanges as distinguished from " spot " exchanges—for enabling the merchant to avoid this risk, not, indeed, during the interval when he is negotiating the contract, but as soon as the negotiation is completed.

Transactions in " spot " exchange are for cash— that is to say, cash in one currency is exchanged for cash in another currency. But merchants who have bought goods in terms of foreign currency for future delivery may not have the cash available pending delivery of the goods ; whilst merchants who have sold goods in terms of foreign currency, but are not yet in a position to sell a draft on the buyer, cannot, even if they have plenty of cash in their own currency, protect themselves by a " spot " sale of the exchange involved, save in the exceptional case when they have cash available in the foreign currency also.

A " forward " contract is for the conclusion of a " spot " transaction in exchanges at a later date, fixed on the basis of the spot rate prevailing at the original date. Pending the date of the maturity of the forward contract no cash need pass (although, of course, the contracting party may be required to give some security or other evidence for his ability to complete the contract in due course), so that the merchant entering into a forward contract is not required to find cash any sooner than if he ran the risk on the exchange until the goods were delivered ; yet he is protected from the consequences of any fluctuation in the exchanges in the meantime.

The tables given below show that in London, in the case of the exchanges which have a big market (the dollar, the franc, and the lira), competition between dealers has brought down the charges for these facilities to a fairly moderate rate. During 1920 and 1921 the cost to an English buyer of foreign currency for forward delivery was a little more expensive than for spot delivery in the case of francs, lire, and marks, and a little cheaper in the case of dollars. Correspondingly, French, Italian, and German merchants were generally in a position to buy both sterling and dollars for forward delivery at a slightly cheaper rate than for spot delivery—that is to say, if they dealt in London. As regards the rates charged in foreign centres my information is not extensive, but it indicates that in Milan, for example, very much less favourable terms for these transactions are frequently charged to the seller of forward sterling than those ruling in London. During 1922, however, the effect of the progressive cheapening of money in London was, for reasons to be explained in a moment, to cheapen the cost to English buyers of foreign currency for forward delivery, forward francs falling to an appreciable discount on spot francs, and forward dollars becoming at the end of the year decidedly cheaper than spot dollars. Later on, the raising of the bank-rate in June 1923 acted again, as could have been predicted, in the opposite direction.

Proceeding to details, we see below (pp. 118, 119) the quotations for forward exchange ruling in the London market since the beginning of 1920. During 1920–21 forward dollars were generally cheaper than spot dollars to a London buyer to the extent of from 1 to $1\frac{1}{2}$ per cent per annum. Occasionally, however, when big movements of the exchange were taking place, the discount on forward dollars was temporarily much higher, having risen, for example,

TABLE OF EXCHANGE QUOTATIONS IN LONDON ONE MONTH FORWARD [1]

Date.	NEW YORK. Spot.	One Month Forward.	Difference per cent per annum.	PARIS. Spot.	One Month Forward.	Difference per cent per annum.
1920						
January .	3·79	+ $\frac{3}{8}$ cent	+1·2	40·90	+ 6 centime	+1·7
February	3·48$\frac{7}{8}$	+ $\frac{1}{4}$,,	+ ·9	46·90	+ 4 ,,	+1·0
March .	3·41$\frac{3}{8}$	+ $\frac{1}{4}$,,	+ ·9	48·55	+ 3 ,,	+ ·7
April .	3·90$\frac{3}{4}$	+ $\frac{3}{8}$,,	+1·2	57·80	+ 3 ,,	+ ·6
May .	3·82$\frac{7}{8}$	+ $\frac{1}{2}$,,	+1·6	64·04	+ 1 ,,	+ ·18
June .	3·89$\frac{1}{16}$	+ $\frac{3}{8}$,,	+1·2	50·45	− 5 ,,	−1·2
July .	3·96$\frac{1}{8}$	+ $\frac{5}{8}$,,	+1·9	47·05	−10 ,,	−2·8
August .	3·67	+ $\frac{1}{2}$,,	+1·6	49·00	−10 ,,	−2·4
September	3·56$\frac{7}{8}$	+ $\frac{1}{2}$,,	+1·7	51·22$\frac{1}{2}$	− 5 ,,	−1·2
October .	3·48$\frac{1}{16}$	+ $\frac{1}{2}$,,	+1·7	52·10	−10 ,,	−2·3
November	3·44$\frac{3}{8}$	+1$\frac{1}{8}$,,	+5·7	54·45	−15 ,,	−3·3
December	3·49	+ $\frac{1}{2}$,,	+1·7	57·45	−15 ,,	−3·2
1921						
January .	3·58$\frac{3}{8}$	+ $\frac{3}{8}$,,	+1·3	61·07$\frac{1}{2}$	−30 ,,	−5·9
February	3·84$\frac{1}{4}$	+1 ,,	+3·1	54·50	−20 ,,	−4·4
March .	3·88$\frac{3}{8}$	+ $\frac{7}{8}$,,	+2·7	54·40	−27 ,,	−5·9
April .	3·92	+ $\frac{3}{8}$,,	+1·1	55·37$\frac{1}{2}$	−15 ,,	−3·3
May .	3·98	+ $\frac{1}{2}$,,	+1·5	50·22$\frac{1}{2}$	−12 ,,	−2·9
June .	3·90$\frac{5}{8}$	+ $\frac{3}{4}$,,	+2·3	46·35	−10 ,,	−2·6
July .	3·71$\frac{11}{16}$	+ $\frac{5}{8}$,,	+2·0	46·72$\frac{1}{2}$	−10 ,,	−2·6
August .	3·56$\frac{3}{8}$	+ $\frac{1}{2}$,,	+1·7	46·77$\frac{1}{2}$	+ 2 ,,	+ ·5
September	3·71$\frac{5}{8}$	+ $\frac{3}{8}$,,	+1·2	48·68$\frac{1}{2}$	+ 3 ,,	+ ·7
October .	3·76$\frac{1}{8}$	+ $\frac{1}{2}$,,	+1·6	52·27$\frac{1}{2}$	+ 1 ,,	+ ·2
November	3·92$\frac{1}{16}$	+ $\frac{7}{8}$,,	+2·7	53·44	+ 4 ,,	+ ·9
December	4·08$\frac{5}{16}$	+ $\frac{3}{8}$,,	+1·1	54·24	+ 2 ,,	+ ·4
1922						
January .	4·20$\frac{1}{8}$	+ $\frac{1}{8}$,,	+ ·4	52·32$\frac{1}{2}$	par	...
February	4·30$\frac{1}{2}$	par	...	51·62$\frac{1}{2}$	,,	...
March .	4·42	,,	...	48·45	,,	...
April .	4·39	,,	...	48·15	− 1 centime	− ·25
May .	4·44$\frac{1}{2}$	,,	...	48·47	+ 1 ,,	+ ·25
June .	4·46$\frac{3}{4}$	+ $\frac{1}{16}$ cent	+ ·5	49·00	+ 2 ,,	+ ·49
July .	4·44$\frac{3}{4}$	+ $\frac{1}{16}$,,	+ ·17	56·20	+ 8 ,,	+1·8
August .	4·45$\frac{1}{4}$	+1$\frac{3}{16}$,,	+ ·5	54·10	+10 ,,	+2·21
September	4·46	+ $\frac{3}{8}$,,	+1	57·40	+ 3 ,,	+ ·63
October .	4·42	+ $\frac{1}{4}$,,	+ ·68	58·25	+ 3 ,,	+ ·62
November	4·46$\frac{1}{2}$	+ $\frac{5}{8}$,,	+1·68	64·65	+14 ,,	+2·59
December	4·51$\frac{3}{4}$	+1 ,,	+2·65	64·30	+ 8 ,,	+1·49
1923						
January .	4·64$\frac{3}{4}$	+1$\frac{1}{4}$,,	+3·23	66·40	+ 5 ,,	+ ·9
February	4·67	+ $\frac{7}{8}$,,	+2·25	75·50	+16 ,,	+2·54
March .	4·70$\frac{5}{8}$	+1 ,,	+2·55	77·50	+11 ,,	+1·70
April .	4·66$\frac{7}{8}$	+ $\frac{3}{4}$,,	+1·93	70·40	+5 ,,	+ ·85
May .	4·62$\frac{1}{2}$	+1$\frac{1}{8}$,,	+2·43	69·35	+5 ,,	+ ·86
June .	4·62$\frac{3}{4}$	+ $\frac{7}{8}$,,	+2·27	71·60	+5 ,,	+ ·84
July .	4·56$\frac{1}{2}$	+ $\frac{1}{2}$,,	+1·31	78·35	+4 ,,	+ ·61
August .	4·57	+ $\frac{1}{4}$,,	+0·66	79·20	+9 ,,	+ ·60

First day of month in 1920, first Wednesday in 1921, and first Friday thereafter.

Table of Exchange Quotations in London One Month Forward

Date.	Italy. Spot.	Italy. One Month Forward.	Italy. Difference per cent per annum.	Germany. Spot.	Germany. One Month Forward.	Germany. Difference per cent per annum.
1920[1]						
January .	50	– $\frac{1}{8}$ lire	– 3·0	187	marks	
February	55	– $\frac{1}{8}$,,	– 2·7	305		
March .	$62\frac{3}{4}$	– $\frac{1}{4}$,,	– 4·7	337		
April .	$80\frac{1}{2}$	– $\frac{1}{4}$,,	– 3·7	275		
May .	83	– $\frac{1}{2}$,,	– 7·1	$218\frac{1}{2}$	– 1 ,,	– 5·5
June .	$66\frac{3}{8}$	– $\frac{1}{2}$,,	– 9·1	$150\frac{1}{2}$	– 1 ,,	– 8·0
July .	$65\frac{3}{8}$	– $\frac{1}{2}$,,	– 9·2	150	– $\frac{1}{2}$,,	– 4·0
August .	70	– $\frac{1}{2}$,,	– 8·5	$160\frac{1}{2}$	– 1 ,,	– 7·5
September	$76\frac{1}{4}$	– $\frac{1}{2}$,,	– 7·9	176	– $\frac{1}{2}$,,	– 3·4
October .	$83\frac{9}{16}$	– $\frac{1}{2}$,,	– 7·2	215	– 1 ,,	– 5·6
November	$93\frac{11}{16}$	– $\frac{1}{2}$,,	– 6·4	$266\frac{1}{2}$	– $\frac{1}{2}$,,	– 2·2
December	$94\frac{13}{16}$	– $\frac{1}{2}$,,	– 6·3	$241\frac{1}{2}$	– 1 ,,	– 4·9
1921						
January .	$104\frac{3}{8}$	par	...	$269\frac{1}{2}$	– 2 ,,	– 8·9
February	$105\frac{1}{2}$	– $\frac{3}{4}$ lire	– 8·5	$243\frac{1}{2}$	– 1 ,,	– 4·9
March .	$106\frac{1}{2}$	– $\frac{5}{8}$,,	– 7·0	$243\frac{1}{2}$	– 1 ,,	– 4·9
April .	$92\frac{1}{4}$	– $\frac{1}{2}$,,	– 6·5	$239\frac{1}{2}$	– 2 ,,	– 10·0
May .	$81\frac{3}{8}$	– $\frac{5}{8}$,,	– 9·1	$262\frac{1}{2}$	– $1\frac{3}{4}$,,	– 8·0
June .	$73\frac{11}{16}$	– $\frac{1}{2}$,,	– 8·1	$245\frac{1}{4}$	– $1\frac{1}{2}$,,	– 7·3
July .	77	– $\frac{1}{2}$,,	– 7·8	$279\frac{1}{2}$	– $1\frac{1}{2}$,,	– 6·45
August .	$85\frac{1}{16}$	– $\frac{1}{4}$,,	– 3·5	286	– 1 ,,	– 4·2
September	$85\frac{9}{16}$	– $\frac{3}{8}$,,	– 5·2	$347\frac{1}{2}$	– $1\frac{1}{2}$,,	– 5·1
October .	$94\frac{1}{8}$	– $\frac{3}{8}$,,	– 4·8	471	– 5 ,,	– 12·7
November	$96\frac{5}{8}$	– $\frac{1}{4}$,,	– 3·1	$764\frac{1}{2}$	– $2\frac{1}{4}$,,	– 3·5
December	$93\frac{15}{16}$	– $\frac{1}{2}$,,	– 6·4	855	– $1\frac{1}{2}$,,	– 2·1
1922						
January .	$97\frac{1}{8}$	– $\frac{1}{4}$,,	– 3·0	$777\frac{1}{2}$	– $3\frac{1}{2}$,,	– 5·4
February	$92\frac{1}{2}$	– $\frac{7}{16}$,,	– 5·7	872	– $2\frac{1}{2}$,,	– 3·4
March .	$83\frac{3}{16}$	– $\frac{1}{4}$,,	– 3·6	1117	– $1\frac{1}{2}$,,	– 1·6
April .	$83\frac{5}{16}$	– 15 pts.	– 2·16	1440	– 8 ,,	– 6·6
May .	83	– 10 ,,	– 1·45	1270	– $\frac{1}{2}$,,	– ·47
June .	$85\frac{7}{8}$	– 3 ,,	– ·41	1222	par	...
July .	100	par	...	2320	+ 5 marks	+ 2·59
August .	96	par	...	3175	+ 20 ,,	+ 7·56
September	101	– 11 ,,	– 1·31	5700	nominal	...
October .	103	– 10 ,,	– 1·16	9900	+ 450 mks	+ 54·54
November	106	– 8 ,,	– ·91	26,250	+ 6,000 ,,	+ 274·3
December	$93\frac{3}{4}$	– 20 ,,	– 2·56	35,000	+ 5,500 ,,	+ 188·58
1923						
January .	92	– 11 ,,	– 1·43	39,500	+ 1,750 ,,	+ 53·16
February	$97\frac{1}{2}$	– 23 ,,	– 2·83	190,000	+ 27,000 ,,	+ 170·53
March .	$97\frac{3}{8}$	– 23 ,,	– 2·82	105,000	+ 10,000 ,,	+ 114·28
April .	$93\frac{3}{4}$	– 18 ,,	– 2·30	97,500	+ 6,000 ,,	+ 73·85
May .	$94\frac{7}{8}$	– 19 ,,	– 2·28	170,000	+ 20,000 ,,	+ 141·18
June .	99	– 15 ,,	– 1·82	350,000	+ 40,000 ,,	+ 137·14
July .	$106\frac{7}{8}$	– 22 ,,	– 2·47	900,000	+ 30,000[1] ,,	+ 40·00
August .	$105\frac{1}{2}$	– 28 ,,	– 3·18	5,500,000	+ 1,500,000[1] ,,	+ 327·27

[1] Nominal.

in November 1920, when sterling was at its lowest point, to nearly 6 per cent—for reasons which I will endeavour to elucidate later. During the first half of 1922 the discount on forward dollars dwindled, but rose again during the latter half of the year, reacting again in the middle of 1923 after money rates in London had been slightly raised. Thus a London merchant, who has had dollar commitments for the purchase of goods, has not only been able to cover his exchange risk by means of a forward transaction, but on the average he has got his exchange a little cheaper by providing for it in advance.

Forward purchases of francs, after being dearer than spot transactions by $2\frac{1}{2}$ per cent per annum or more from the middle of 1920 to the middle of 1921, were nearly level in price from the middle of 1921 to the middle of 1922, whilst since that time they have been $\frac{1}{2}$ to $2\frac{1}{2}$ per cent per annum cheaper. In the case of lire there have been much wider gaps, forward purchases being frequently 3 per cent or more dearer than spot. In the case of German marks, the forward rate, after ranging round about 5 per cent per annum dearer than spot, has reached, since the autumn of 1922 and the complete collapse of the mark, a figure fantastically cheaper, thus reflecting the sensational rate of interest for short loans current inside Germany.

But in all these cases (except in Germany since the complete collapse of the mark), whether for-

ward exchange is at a discount or at a premium
on spot, the expense, if any, of dealing forward
has been small in relation to the risks that are
avoided.

Nevertheless, in practice merchants do not avail
themselves of these facilities to the extent that might
have been expected. The nature of forward dealings
in exchange is not generally understood. The rates
are seldom quoted in the newspapers. There are few
financial topics of equal importance which have
received so little discussion or publicity. The present
situation did not exist before the war (although
even at that time forward rates for the dollar were
regularly quoted), and did not begin until after the
"unpegging" of the leading exchanges in 1919, so
that the business world has only begun to adapt itself.
Moreover, for the ordinary man, dealing in forward
exchange has, it seems, a smack of speculation about
it. Unlike Manchester cotton spinners, who have
learnt by long experience that it is not the hedging
of open cotton commitments on the Liverpool futures
market, but the failure to do so, which is speculative,
merchants, who buy or sell goods of which the price
is expressed in a foreign currency, do not yet regard
it as part of the normal routine of prudent business
to hedge these indirect exchange commitments by
a transaction in forward exchange.

It is important, on the other hand, not to exaggerate
the extent to which, at the present time, merchants

can by this means protect themselves from risk. In the first place, for reasons, some of which will be considered below, it is only in certain of the leading exchanges that these transactions can be carried out at a reasonable charge. It is not clear that even the banks themselves have yet learnt to look on the provision for their clients of such facilities at fair and reasonable rates as one of the most useful services they can offer. They have been too much influenced, perhaps, by the fear that these facilities might tend at the same time to increase speculation.

But there is a further qualification, not to be overlooked, to the value of forward transactions as a protection against risk. The price of a particular commodity, in terms of a particular currency, does not exactly respond to changes in the value of that currency on the exchange markets of the world, with the result that a movement in a country's exchanges may, in the case of a commodity of which that country is a large seller or a large purchaser, change the commodity's world-value expressed in terms of gold. In that case a merchant, even though he is hedged in respect of the exchange itself, may lose, in respect of his unsold trading stocks, through a movement in the world-value of the commodity he is dealing in, directly occasioned by the exchange fluctuation.

If we turn to the theoretical analysis of the

forward market, what is it that determines the amount and the sign (whether plus or minus) of the divergence between the spot and forward rates as recorded above ?

If dollars one month forward are quoted cheaper than spot dollars to a London buyer in terms of sterling, this indicates a preference by the market, on balance, in favour of holding funds in New York during the month in question rather than in London, —a preference the degree of which is measured by the discount on forward dollars. For if spot dollars are worth \$4.40 to the pound and dollars one month forward \$4.40½ to the pound, then the owner of \$4.40 can, by selling the dollars spot and buying them back one month forward, find himself at the end of the month with \$4.40½, merely by being during the month the owner of £1 in London instead of \$4.40 in New York. That he should require and can obtain half a cent, which, earned in one month, is equal to about 1½ per cent per annum, to induce him to do the transaction, shows, and is, under conditions of competition, a measure of, the market's preference for holding funds during the month in question in New York rather than in London.

Conversely, if francs, lire, and marks one month forward are quoted dearer than the spot rates to a London buyer, this indicates a preference for holding funds in London rather than in Paris, Rome, or Berlin.

The difference between the spot and forward rates is, therefore, precisely and exactly the measure of the preference of the money and exchange market for holding funds in one international centre rather than in another, *the exchange risk apart*, that is to say under conditions in which the exchange risk is covered. What is it that determines these preferences ?

1. The most fundamental cause is to be found in the interest rates obtainable on " short " money— that is to say, on money lent or deposited for short periods of time in the money markets of the two centres under comparison. If by lending dollars in New York for one month the lender could earn interest at the rate of $5\frac{1}{2}$ per cent per annum, whereas by lending sterling in London for one month he could only earn interest at the rate of 4 per cent, then the preference observed above for holding funds in New York rather than in London is wholly explained. That is to say, forward quotations for the purchase of the currency of the dearer money market tend to be cheaper than spot quotations by a percentage per month equal to the excess of the interest which can be earned in a month in the dearer market over what can be earned in the cheaper. It must be noticed that the governing factor is the rate of interest obtainable for short periods, so that a country where, owing to the absence or ill-development of an organised money market, it is difficult to lend

money satisfactorily at call or for very short periods, may, for the purposes of this calculation, reckon as a low interest-earning market, even though the prevailing rate of interest for longer periods is not low at all. This consideration generally tends to make London and New York more attractive markets for short money than any Continental centres.

The effect of the cheap money rates ruling in London from the middle of 1922 to the middle of 1923 in diminishing the attractiveness of London as a depository of funds is strikingly shown, in the above tables, by the cheapening of the forward quotations of foreign currencies relatively to the spot quotations. In the case of the dollar the forward quotation had risen by the beginning of 1923 to a rate 3 per cent per annum above the spot quotation (*i.e.* forward dollars were 3 per cent per annum *cheaper* than spot dollars in terms of sterling), which meant (subject to modification by the other influences to be mentioned below) that the effective rate for short loans approached 3 per cent higher in New York than in London.

In the case of francs forward quotations which had been below spot, so long as money was dear in London, rose above the spot quotations, thus indicating that the relative dearness of money in London as compared with Paris had disappeared ; whilst in the case of lire forward quotations, although still below spot quotations, rose, under the same influence, nearer to the spot level. Nevertheless, in the case of both these currencies, a preponderance of bearish anticipations about their future prospects probably also played a part, for the reasons given in detail below, in producing the observed result.

The most interesting figures, however, are those relating to marks, which illustrate vividly what I have mentioned on page 23 above concerning the enormous money rates of interest current in Germany subsequent to the collapse of October 1922, as a result of the effort of the real rate of interest to remain positive in face of a general anticipation of a catastrophic collapse of the monetary unit. It will be noticed that the effective short money rate of interest in terms of marks ranged from 50 per cent per annum upwards, until finally the quotations were merely nominal.

2. If questions of credit did not enter in, the factor of the rate of interest on short loans would be the dominating one. Indeed, as between London and New York, it probably is so under existing conditions. Between London and Paris it is still important. But elsewhere the various uncertainties of financial and political risk, which the war has left behind, introduce a further element which sometimes quite transcends the factor of relative interest. The possibility of financial trouble or political disturbance, and the quite appreciable probability of a moratorium in the event of any difficulties arising, or of the sudden introduction of

exchange regulations which would interfere with the
movement of balances out of the country, and even
sometimes the contingency of a drastic demonetisation,
—all these factors deter bankers, even when the
exchange risk proper is eliminated, from maintaining
large floating balances at certain foreign centres.
Such risks prevent the business from being based,
as it should be, on a mathematical calculation of
interest rates; they obliterate by their possible
magnitude the small "turns" which can be earned
out of differences between interest rates plus a normal
banker's commission; and, being incalculable, they
may even deter conservative bankers from doing
the business on a substantial scale at any reasonable
rate at all. In the case of Roumania or Poland,
for example, this factor is, at times, the dominating
one.

3. There is a third factor of some significance.
We have assumed so far that the forward rate is
fixed at such a level that the dealer or banker can
cover himself by a simultaneous spot transaction
and be left with a reasonable profit for his trouble.
But it is not necessary to cover every forward transaction by a corresponding spot transaction; it may
be possible to "marry" a forward sale with a forward
purchase of the same currency. For example, whilst
some of the market's clients may wish to sell forward
dollars, other clients will wish to buy forward dollars.
In this case the market can set off these, one against

the other, in its books, and there will be no need of any movement of cash funds in either direction. The third factor depends, therefore, on whether it is the sellers or the buyers of forward dollars who predominate. To fix our minds, let us suppose that money-market conditions exist in which a sale of forward dollars against the purchase of spot dollars, at a discount of $1\frac{1}{2}$ per cent per annum for the former, yields neither profit nor loss. Now if in these conditions the purchasers of forward dollars, other than arbitragers, exceed sellers of forward dollars, then this excess of demand for forward dollars can be met by arbitragers, who have cash resources in London, at a discount which falls short of $1\frac{1}{2}$ per cent per annum by such amount (say $\frac{1}{2}$ per cent) as will yield the arbitragers sufficient profit for their trouble. If, however, sellers of forward dollars exceed the purchasers, then a sufficient discount has to be accepted by the former to induce arbitrage the other way round—that is to say, by arbitragers who have cash resources in New York—namely, a discount which exceeds $1\frac{1}{2}$ per cent per annum by, say, $\frac{1}{2}$ per cent. Thus the discount on forward dollars will fluctuate between 1 and 2 per cent per annum according as buyers or sellers predominate.

4. Lastly, we have to provide for the case, quite frequent in practice, where our assumption of a large and free market breaks down. A business in forward exchange can only be transacted by banks or similar

institutions. If the bulk of the business in a particular
exchange is in a few hands, or if there is a tacit
agreement between the principal institutions concerned to maintain differences which will allow more
than a competitive profit, then the surcharge representing the profit of a bank for arbitraging between
spot and forward transactions may much exceed
the moderate figure indicated above. The quotations of the rates charged in Milan for forward
dealings in lire, when compared with the rates
current in London at the same date, indicate that
a bank which is free to operate in both markets
can frequently make an abnormal profit.

But there is a further contingency of considerable
importance which occurs when speculation is exceptionally active and is all one way. It must be
remembered that the floating capital normally available, and ready to move from centre to centre for
the purpose of taking advantage of moderate arbitrage
profits between spot and forward exchange, is by
no means unlimited in amount, and is not always
adequate to the market's requirements. When, for
example, the market is feeling unusually bullish of
the European exchanges as against sterling, or of
sterling as against dollars, the pressure to sell forward
sterling or dollars, as the case may be, may drive
the forward price of these currencies to a discount
on their spot price which represents an altogether
abnormal profit to any one who is in a position to

buy these currencies forward and sell them spot.
This abnormal discount can only disappear when the
high profit of arbitrage between spot and forward
has drawn fresh capital into the arbitrage business.
So few persons understand even the elements of
the theory of the forward exchanges that there
was an occasion in 1920, even between London and
New York, when a seller of spot dollars could earn
at the rate of 6 per cent per annum above the London
rate for short money by converting his dollars into
sterling and providing at the same time by a forward
sale of the sterling for reconversion into dollars in a
month's time ; whilst, according to figures supplied
me, it was possible, at the end of February 1921,
by selling spot sterling in Milan and buying it back
a month forward, to earn at the rate of more than
25 per cent per annum over and above any interest
obtainable on a month's deposit of cash lire in Milan.

It is interesting to notice that when the differences
between forward and spot rates have become temporarily abnormal, thus indicating an exceptional
pressure of speculative activity, the speculators
have often turned out to be right. For example,
the abnormal discount on forward dollars, which
persisted more or less from November 1920 to
February 1921, thus indicating that the market was
a bull of sterling, coincided with the sensational
rise of sterling from 3.45 to 3.90. This discount was
at its maximum when sterling touched its lowest

point and at its minimum (in the middle of May 1921) when sterling reached its highest point on that swing, which showed a remarkably accurate anticipation of events by the balance of professional opinion. The comparatively high discount on forward dollars current at the end of 1922 may, in the same way, have been partly due to an excess of bull speculation in favour of sterling based on an expectation of its recovery towards par, and not merely to the cheapness of money in London as compared with New York.

The same thing seems to have been true for the franc. In January and February 1921, the abnormal premium on the forward franc indicated that, in the view of the market, the franc had fallen too low, which turned out to be the case. They turned round at the precise moment when the franc reached its highest value (end of July 1921), and were right again. During the first five months of 1922, when the franc was almost stable, spot and forward quotations were practically at par with one another, whilst the progressive fall of the franc since June 1922 has been accompanied by a steady and sometimes substantial discount on forward francs; indicating, on this test, that the professional market was bearish of francs and therefore right once more. The lira tells somewhat the same tale. Thus, whilst the reader can see for himself by a study of the tables that no precise generalisation would be accurate, nevertheless the market has been broadly right when it has taken a very decided view, as measured by forward rates.

This result may seem surprising in view of the huge amounts which exchange speculators in European currencies, more particularly on the bull side, are reputed to have lost. But the mass of amateur speculators throughout the world operate by cash purchases of the currency of which they are bulls, forward transactions being neither known nor available to them. Such speculation may afford temporary support to the spot exchange, but it has no influence on the difference between spot and forward, the subject now under discussion. The above conclusion is limited to the fact that when the type of professional speculation which makes use of the forward market is exceptionally active and united in its opinion, it has proved roughly correct, and has, therefore, been a useful factor in moderating the extreme fluctuations which would have occurred otherwise.

Out of the various practical conclusions which might be drawn from this discussion and the figures which accompany it, I will pick out three.

1. Those exchanges in which the fluctuations are wildest and the merchant is most in need of facilities for hedging his risk are precisely those in which facilities for forward dealing at moderate rates are

least developed. But this is to be explained, not necessarily by the instability of the exchange in itself, but by certain accompanying circumstances, such as distrust of the country's internal arrangements or its banking credit, a fear of the sudden imposition of exchange regulations or of a moratorium, and the other analogous influences mentioned above (pp. 126-7). There is no theoretical reason why there should not be an excellent forward market in a highly unstable exchange. In those countries, therefore, where regulation is still premature, it may nevertheless be possible to mitigate the evil consequences of fluctuation by organising facilities for forward dealings.

This is a function which the State banks of such countries could usefully perform. For this they must either themselves command a certain amount of foreign currency or they must provide facilities for accepting short-period deposits in their own currency from foreign bankers, on conditions which inspire these bankers with complete confidence in the freedom and liquidity of such deposits. Various technical devices could be suggested. But the simplest method might be for the State banks themselves to enter the forward market and offer to buy or sell forward exchange at a reasonable discount or premium on the spot quotation. I suggest that they should deal not direct with the public but only with approved banks and financial houses, from whom they should require adequate security ; that they should quote every day their rates for buying and selling exchange either one or three months forward ; but that such quotation should take the form, not of a price for the exchange itself, but of a percentage difference between spot and forward, and should be a quotation for the double transaction of a spot deal one way and a simultaneous forward deal the other—*e.g.* the Bank of Italy might offer to sell spot sterling and buy forward sterling at a premium of $\frac{1}{8}$ per cent per month for the former over the latter, and to buy spot sterling and sell forward sterling at par. For the transaction of such business the State banks would require to command a certain amount of resources abroad, either in cash or in borrowing facilities. But this fund would be a revolving one, automatically replenished at the maturity of the forward contracts, so that it need not be on anything like the scale necessary for a fund for the purpose of supporting the exchange. Nor is it a business which involves any more risk than is inherent in all banking business as such ; from exchange risk proper is free.

With free forward markets thus established no merchant need run an exchange risk unless he wishes to, and business might find a stable foothold even in a fluctuating world. A recommendation in favour of action along these lines was included amongst the Financial Resolutions of the Genoa Conference of 1922.

I shall develop below (Chap. V.) a proposal that
the Bank of England should strengthen its control by
fixing spot and forward prices for gold every Thursday
just as it now fixes its discount rate. But other
Central Banks also would increase their control over
fluctuations in exchange if they were to adopt the
above plan of quoting rates for forward exchange in
terms of spot exchange. By varying these rates
they would be able, in effect, to vary the interest
offered for *foreign* balances, as a policy distinct from
whatever might be their bank-rate policy for the
purpose of governing the interest obtainable on *home*
balances.

2. It is not unusual at present for banks to
endeavour to distinguish between speculative dealings
in forward exchange and dealings which are intended
to hedge a commercial transaction, with a view to
discouraging the former; whilst official exchange
regulations in many countries have been aimed at
such discrimination. I think that this is a mistake.
Banks should take stringent precautions to make
sure that their clients are in a position to meet any
losses which may accrue without serious embarrassment. But, having fully assured themselves on this
point, it is not useful that they should inquire further
—for the following reasons.

In the first place, it is almost impossible to prevent
the evasion of such regulations; whilst, if the business
is driven to methods of evasion, it tends to be pressed

underground, to yield excessive profits to middlemen, and to fall into undesirable hands.

But, what is more important and is less appreciated, the speculator with resources can provide a useful, indeed almost an essential, service. Since the volume of actual trade is spread unevenly through the year, the seasonal fluctuation, as explained above, is bound to occur with undue force unless some financial, non-commercial factor steps in to balance matters. A free forward market, from which speculative transactions are not excluded, will give by far the best facilities for the trader, who does not wish to speculate, to avoid doing so. The same sort of advantages will be secured for merchants generally as are afforded, for example, to the cotton trade by the dealings in " futures " in the New York and Liverpool markets. Where risk is unavoidably present, it is much better that it should be carried by those who are qualified or are desirous to bear it, than by traders, who have neither the qualification nor the desire to do so, and whose minds it distracts from their own business. The wide fluctuations in the leading exchanges over the past three years, as distinct from their persisting depreciation, have been due, not to the presence of speculation, but to the absence of a sufficient volume of it relatively to the volume of trade.

3. A failure to analyse the relation between spot and forward exchange may be, sometimes, partly responsible for a mistaken bank-rate policy. Dear

money—that is to say, high interest rates for short-period loans—has two effects. The one is indirect and gradual—namely, in diminishing the volume of credit quoted by the banks. This effect is much the same now as it always was. It is desirable to produce it when prices are rising and business is trying to expand faster than the supply of real capital and effective demand can permit in the long run. It is undesirable when prices are falling and trade is depressed.

The other effect of dear money, or rather of dearer money in one centre than in another, used to be to draw gold from the cheaper centre for temporary employment in the dearer. But nowadays the only immediate effect is to cause a new adjustment of the difference between the spot and forward rates of exchange between the two centres. If money becomes dearer in London, the discount on forward dollars diminishes or gives way to a premium. The effect has been pointed out above of the relative cheapening of money in London in the latter half of 1922 in increasing the discount on forward dollars, and of the relative raising of money-rates in the middle of 1923 in diminishing the discount. Such are, in present circumstances, the principal direct consequences of a moderate difference between interest rates in the two centres, apart, of course, from the indirect, long-period influence. Since no one is likely to remit money temporarily from one money market to another on any important scale, with an uncovered exchange risk, merely to take advantage of $\frac{1}{2}$ or 1 per cent per annum difference in the interest rate, the direct effect of dearer money on the *absolute* level of the exchanges, as distinguished from the difference between spot and forward, is very small, being limited to the comparatively slight influence which the relation between spot and forward rates exerts on exchange speculators.[1] The pressure of arbitragers between spot and forward exchange, seeking to take advantage of the new situation, leads to a rapid adjustment of the difference between these rates, until the business of temporary remittance, as distinct from exchange speculation, is no more profitable than it was before, and consequently does not occur on any increased scale ; with the result that there is no marked effect on the absolute level of the spot rate.

The reasons given for the maintenance of a close relationship between the Bank of England's rate and that of the American Federal Reserve Board sometimes show confusion. The eventual influence of an effective high bank-rate on the general situation is undisputed ; but the belief that a moderate differ-

---

[1] If interest rates are raised in London, the discount on forward dollars will decrease or a premium will appear. This is likely to have some influence in encouraging speculative sales of forward dollars (how much influence depends on the proportion borne by the difference between the spot and forward rates to the probable range of fluctuation of the spot rate which the speculator anticipates) ; and in so far as this is the case, the covering sales of spot dollars by banks will move the rate of exchange in favour of London.

ence between bank-rates in London and New York reacts directly on the sterling-dollar exchange, as it used to do under a régime of convertibility, is a misapprehension. The direct reaction of this difference is on the discount for forward dollars as against spot dollars ; and it cannot much affect the absolute level of the spot rate unless the change in relative money-rates is comparable in magnitude (as it used to be but no longer is) with the possible range of exchange fluctuations.

CHAPTER IV

ALTERNATIVE AIMS IN MONETARY POLICY

OUR first two chapters, on the evils proceeding from instability in the purchasing power of money and on the part played by the exigencies of Public Finance, have indicated the practical importance of our subject to the welfare of society. In the third chapter an attempt has been made to lay a foundation of theory upon which to raise constructions. We can now turn, in this and the following chapter, to *Remedies*.

The instability of money has been compounded, in most countries except the United States, of two elements : the failure of the national currencies to remain stable in terms of what was supposed to be the standard of value, namely gold ; and the failure of gold itself to remain stable in terms of purchasing power. Attention has been mainly concentrated (*e.g.* by the Cunliffe Committee) on the first of these two factors. It is often assumed that the restoration of the gold standard, that is to say, of the convertibility of each national currency at a fixed rate in terms of gold, must be, in any case, our objective ;

and that the main question of controversy is whether national currencies should be restored to their pre-war gold value or to some lower value nearer to the present facts ; in other words, the choice between *Deflation* and *Devaluation*.

This assumption is hasty. If we glance at the course of prices during the last five years, it is obvious that the United States, which has enjoyed a gold standard throughout, has suffered as severely as many other countries, that in the United Kingdom the instability of gold has been a larger factor than the instability of the exchange, that the same is true even of France, and that in Italy it has been nearly as large. On the other hand, in India, which has suffered violent exchange fluctuations, the standard of value, as we shall see below, has been more stable than in any other country.

We should not, therefore, by fixing the exchanges get rid of our currency troubles. It is even possible that this step might weaken our control. The problem of stabilisation has several sides, which we must consider one by one :

1. Devaluation *versus* Deflation. Do we wish to fix the standard of value, whether or not it be gold, near the existing value ? Or do we wish to restore it to the pre-war value ?

2. Stability of Prices *versus* Stability of Exchange. Is it more important that the value of a national currency should be stable in terms of purchasing

power, or stable in terms of the currency of certain foreign countries ?

3. The Restoration of a Gold Standard. In the light of our answers to the first two questions, is a gold standard, however imperfect in theory, the best available method for attaining our ends in practice ?

Having decided between these alternative aims, we can proceed, in the next chapter, to some constructive suggestions.

I. *Devaluation* versus *Deflation.*

The policy of reducing the ratio between the volume of a country's currency and its requirements of purchasing power in the form of money, so as to increase the exchange value of the currency in terms of gold or of commodities, is conveniently called *Deflation*.

The alternative policy of stabilising the value of the currency somewhere near its present value, without regard to its pre-war value, is called *Devaluation*.

Up to the date of the Genoa Conference of April 1922, these two policies were not clearly distinguished by the public, and the sharp opposition between them has been only gradually appreciated. Even now (October 1923) there is scarcely any European country in which the authorities have made it clear whether their policy is to stabilise the value of their currency or to raise it. Stabilisation at the existing level has been recommended by International Conferences ;[1] and the actual value of many currencies tends to fall rather than to rise. But, to judge from other indications, the heart's desire of the State Banks of Europe, whether they pursue it successfully, as in Czecho-Slovakia, or unsuccessfully, as in France, is to *raise* the value of their currencies. In only one country so far have practical steps been taken to *fix* the exchange, namely in Austria.

The simple arguments against Deflation fall under two heads.

In the first place, Deflation is not *desirable*, because ¡t effects, what is always harmful, a change in the existing Standard of Value, and redistributes wealth in a manner injurious, at the same time, to business and to social stability. Deflation, as we have already seen, involves a transference of wealth from the rest of the community to the *rentier* class and to all holders of titles to money ; just as inflation involves the opposite. In particular it involves a transference from all borrowers, that is to say from traders, manufacturers, and farmers, to lenders, from the active to the inactive.

---

[1] Whilst the Conference of Genoa (April 1922) affirmed the doctrine in general, representatives of the countries chiefly affected were united in declaring that it must not be applied to them in particular. Signor Peano, M. Picard, and M. Theunis, speaking on behalf of Italy, France, and Belgium, announced, each for his own country, that they would have nothing to do with devaluating, and were determined to restore their respective currencies to their pre-war values. Reform is not likely to come by joint, simultaneous action. The experts of Genoa recognised this when they " ventured to suggest " that " a considerable service will be rendered by that country which first decides boldly to set the example of securing immediate stability in terms of gold " by devaluation.

But whilst the oppression of the taxpayer for the enrichment of the *rentier* is the chief lasting result, there is another, more violent, disturbance during the period of transition. The policy of gradually raising the value of a country's money to (say) 100 per cent above its present value in terms of goods—I repeat here the arguments of Chapter I.—amounts to giving notice to every merchant and every manufacturer, that for some time to come his stock and his raw materials will steadily depreciate on his hands, and to every one who finances his business with borrowed money that he will, sooner or later, lose 100 per cent on his liabilities (since he will have to pay back in terms of commodities twice as much as he has borrowed). Modern business, being carried on largely with borrowed money, must necessarily be brought to a standstill by such a process. It will be to the interest of every one in business to go out of business for the time being; and of every one who is contemplating expenditure to postpone his orders so long as he can. The wise man will be he who turns his assets into cash, withdraws from the risks and the exertions of activity, and awaits in country retirement the steady appreciation promised him in the value of his cash. A probable expectation of Deflation is bad enough; a certain expectation is disastrous. For the mechanism of the modern business world is even less adapted to fluctuations in the value of money upwards than it is to fluctuations downwards.

In the second place, in many countries, Deflation, even were it desirable, is not *possible*; that is to say, Deflation in sufficient degree to restore the currency to its pre-war parity. For the burden which it would throw on the taxpayer would be insupportable. I need add nothing on this to what I have already written in the second chapter above. This practical impossibility might have rendered the policy innocuous, if it were not that, by standing in the way of the alternative policy, it prolongs the period of uncertainty and severe seasonal fluctuation, and even, in some cases, can be carried into effect sufficiently to cause much interference with business. The fact, that the restoration of their currencies to the pre-war parity is still the declared official policy of the French and Italian Governments, is preventing, in those countries, any rational discussion of currency reform. All those — and in the financial world they are many—who have reasons for wishing to appear "correct," are compelled to talk foolishly. In Italy, where sound economic views have much influence and which may be nearly ripe for currency reform, Signor Mussolini has threatened to raise the lira to its former value. Fortunately for the Italian taxpayer and Italian business, the lira does not listen even to a dictator and cannot be given castor oil. But such talk can postpone positive reform; though it may be doubted if so good a politician would have propounded such a policy, even in bravado and exuberance, if he had understood that, expressed in other but equivalent words, it was as follows : " My policy is to halve wages, double the burden of the National Debt, and to reduce by 50 per cent the prices which Sicily can get for her exports of oranges and lemons."

One single country—Czechoslovakia—has made the experiment on a modest but sufficient scale. Comparatively free from the burden of internal debt, and free also from serious budgetary deficits, Czechoslovakia was able in the course of 1922, in pursuance of the policy of her Finance Minister, Dr. Alois Rasin, to employ the proceeds of certain foreign loans to improve the exchange value of the Czech crown to nearly three times the rate which had been touched in the previous year. The policy has cost her an industrial crisis and serious unemployment. To what purpose ? I do not know. Even now the Czech crown is not worth a sixth of its pre-war parity ; and it remains unstabilised, fluttering before the breath of the seasons and the wind of politics. Is, therefore, the process of appreciation to continue indefinitely ? If not, when and at what point is stabilisation to be effected ? Czechoslovakia was better placed than any country in Europe to establish her economic life on the basis of a sound and fixed currency. Her finances were in equilibrium, her credit good, her foreign resources adequate, and no one could have blamed her for devaluating the crown, ruined by no fault of hers

and inherited from the Habsburg Empire. Pursuing
a misguided policy in a spirit of stern virtue, she
preferred the stagnation of her industries and a still
fluctuating standard.[1]

If the restoration of many European currencies
to their pre-war parity with gold is neither desirable
nor possible, what are the forces or the arguments
which have established this undesirable impossibility
as the avowed policy of most of them ?   The following
are the most important :

1. *To leave the gold value of a country's currency at
the low level to which war has driven it is an injustice
to the rentier class and to others whose income is fixed
in terms of currency, and practically a breach of
contract ; whilst to restore its value would meet a
debt of honour.*

The injury done to pre-war holders of fixed interest-
bearing stocks is beyond dispute.   Real justice, indeed,
might require the restoration of the purchasing power,

---

[1] I cannot criticise the work, in his second term of office (1922), of
Dr. Rasin, now fallen by the hand of an assassin, without reference to his
great achievement during his first term (1919) in rescuing his country's
currency from the surrounding chaos.   The stamping of the Austrian
notes and the levy on holders of titles to money which accompanied it
was the only drastic, courageous, and successful measure of finance carried
through anywhere in Europe at that epoch ; the story of it from Dr.
Rasin's own pen can be read in his *The Financial Policy of Czecho-Slovakia*.
Before he had finished other influences became dominant.   But, when in
1922 this austere and disinterested Minister returned to office, he missed,
in my judgment, his opportunity.   He could have completed his task by
establishing the currency on a fixed and stable basis, instead of which
he used his great authority to disorder trade by a futile process of Deflation.

and not merely the gold value, of their money incomes, a measure which no one in fact proposes ; whilst nominal justice has not been infringed, since these investments were not in gold bullion but in the legal tender of the realm. Nevertheless, if this class of investors could be dealt with separately, considerations of equity and the expedience of satisfying reasonable expectation would furnish a strong case.

But this is not the actual situation. The vast issues of War Loans have swamped the pre-war holdings of fixed interest-bearing stocks, and society has largely adjusted itself to the new situation. To restore the value of pre-war holdings by Deflation means enhancing at the same time the value of war and post-war holdings, and thereby raising the total claims of the *rentier* class not only beyond what they are entitled to, but to an intolerable proportion of the total income of the community. Indeed justice, rightly weighed, comes down on the other side. Much the greater proportion of the money contracts still outstanding were entered into when money was worth more nearly what it is worth now than what it was worth in 1913. Thus, in order to do justice to a minority of creditors, a great injustice would be done to a great majority of debtors.

This aspect of the matter has been admirably argued by Professor Irving Fisher.[1] We forget, he

---

[1] In his article " Devaluation *versus* Deflation," published in the eleventh *Manchester Guardian* Reconstruction Supplement (Dec. 7, 1922).

says, that not all contracts require the same adjustment in order to secure justice, and that while we are debating whether we ought to deflate to secure ideal justice for those who made contracts on old price levels, new contracts are constantly being made at the new price levels. An estimate of the volume of contracts now outstanding, classified according to their age, would show that some contracts are a day old, some are a month old, some are a year old, some are a decade old, and some are a century old, the great mass, however, being of very recent origin. Consequently the average, or centre of gravity, of the total existing indebtedness is probably always somewhat near the present. Before the war, Professor Fisher estimated, very roughly, that contracts in the United States were on the average about one year old.

When, therefore, the depreciation of the currency has lasted long enough for society to adjust itself to the new values, Deflation is even worse than Inflation. Both are "unjust" and disappoint reasonable expectation. But whereas Inflation, by easing the burden of national debt and stimulating enterprise, has a little to throw into the other side of the balance, Deflation has nothing.

2. *The restoration of a currency to its pre-war gold value enhances a country's financial prestige and promotes future confidence.*

Where a country can hope to restore its pre-war parity at an early date, this argument cannot be neglected. This might be said of Great Britain, Holland, Sweden, Switzerland, and (perhaps) Spain, but of no other European country. The argument cannot be extended to those countries which, even if they could raise somewhat the value of their legal-tender money, could not possibly restore it to its old value. It is of the essence of the argument that the *exact* pre-war parity should be recovered. It would not make much difference to the financial prestige of Italy whether she stabilised the lira at 100 to the £ sterling or at 60; and it would be much better for her prestige to stabilise it definitely at 100 than to let it fluctuate between 60 and 100.

This argument is limited, therefore, to those countries the gold value of whose currencies is within (say) 5 or 10 per cent of their former value. Its force in these cases depends, I think, upon what answer we give to the problem discussed below, namely, whether we intend to pin ourselves in the future, as in the past, to an unqualified gold standard. If we still prefer such a standard to any available alternative, and if future "confidence" in our currency is to depend not on the stability of its purchasing power but on the fixity of its gold-value, then it may be worth our while to stand the racket of Deflation to the extent of 5 or 10 per cent. This view is in accordance with that expressed by Ricardo in analogous circumstances a hundred years ago.[1] If,

---

[1] See below, p. 153.

on the other hand, we decide to aim for the future
at stability of the price level rather than at a fixed
parity with gold, in that case *cadit quaestio*.

In any case this argument does not affect our
main conclusion, that the right policy for countries
of which the currency has suffered a prolonged and
severe depreciation is to *devaluate*, and to fix the
value of the currency at that figure in the neighbourhood of the existing value to which commerce and
wages are adjusted.

3. *If the gold value of a country's currency can be
increased, labour will profit by a reduced cost of living,
foreign goods will be obtainable cheaper, and foreign
debts fixed in terms of gold* (e.g. *to the United States*)
will be discharged with less effort.

This argument, which is pure delusion, exercises
quite as much influence as the other two. If the
franc is worth more, wages, it is argued, which are
paid in francs, will surely buy more, and French
imports, which are paid for in francs, will be so much
cheaper. No! If francs are worth more they will
buy more labour as well as more goods,—that is to
say, wages will fall ; and the French exports, which
pay for the imports, will, measured in francs, fall in
value just as much as the imports. Nor will it make
in the long run any difference whatever in the amount
of goods the value of which England will have to
transfer to America to pay her dollar debts, whether
in the end sterling settles down at four dollars to

the pound, or at its pre-war parity. The burden of
this debt depends on the value of gold, in terms of
which it is fixed, not on the value of sterling. It is
not easy, it seems, for men to apprehend that their
money is a mere intermediary, without significance
in itself, which flows from one hand to another, is
received and is dispensed, and disappears when its
work is done from the sum of a nation's wealth.

In concluding this section, let me quote on the
issue between Deflation and Devaluation two classic
authorities, Gibbon and Ricardo, the one to represent
the imposing but false wisdom of the would-be
upright statesman, the other to speak in clear tones
the voice of instructed reason.

In the eleventh chapter of *The Decline and Fall*,
Gibbon deems incredible a story of how in A.D. 274
Aurelian's deflationary zeal to restore the integrity
of the coin excited an insurrection which caused
the death of 7000 soldiers. "We might naturally
expect," he says, "that the reformation of the coin
should have been an action equally popular with the
destruction of those obsolete accounts, which by the
emperor's order were burnt in the forum of Trajan.
In an age when the principles of commerce were so
imperfectly understood, the most desirable end might
perhaps be effected by harsh and injudicious means ;
but a temporary grievance of such a nature can
scarcely excite and support a serious civil war. The

repetition of intolerable taxes, imposed either on the land or on the necessaries of life, may at last provoke those who will not or who cannot relinquish their country. But the case is far otherwise in every operation which, by whatsoever expedients, restores the just value of money."

Rome may have understood the principles of commerce imperfectly in the third century and not perfectly in the twentieth; but that does not save her citizens from experiencing their applications. Signor Mussolini might peruse with interest the annals of Aurelian, who, " ignorant or impatient of the restraints of civil institutions," fell by the hand of an assassin within a year of his deflation of the currency, " regretted by the army, detested by the Senate, but universally acknowledged as a warlike and fortunate prince, the useful though severe reformer of a degenerate State."

Ricardo, speaking in the House of Commons on the 12th of June 1822,[1] gave his opinion that: " If in the year 1819 the value of the currency had stood at 14s. for the pound note, which was the case in the year 1813, he should have thought that, on a balance of all the advantages and disadvantages of the case,

[1] The great debate of June 11 and 12, 1822, on Mr. Western's Motion concerning the Resumption of Cash Payments, well illustrates, more particularly in the speeches of the opener, Mr. Western, and of the opposer, Mr. Huskisson, the regularity of the evils which follow a deflationary raising of the standard, and the unchanging antithesis between the temperaments of deflationists and devaluers, though I doubt if any present-day deflationists could make a speech at the same time so able and so unfair as Mr. Huskisson's.

it would have been as well to fix the currency at the then value, according to which most of the existing contracts had been made ; but when the currency was within 5 per cent of its par value, he thought they had made the best selection in recurring to the old standard."

The same is repeated in his *Protection to Agriculture*,[1] where he approves the restoration of the old standard when gold was £4 : 2s. per standard ounce, but adds that, if it had been £5 : 10s., " no measure could have been more inexpedient than to make so violent a change in all subsisting engagements."

II. *Stability of Prices* versus *Stability of Exchange*.

Since, subject to the qualification of Chapter III., the rate of exchange of a country's currency with the currency of the rest of the world (assuming for the sake of simplicity that there is only one external currency) depends on the relation between the internal price level and the external price level, it follows that the exchange cannot be stable unless *both* internal *and* external price levels remain stable. If, therefore, the external price level lies outside our control, we must submit either to our own internal price level or to our exchange being pulled about by external influences. If the external price level is unstable, we cannot keep *both* our own price level

[1] *Works*, p. 468.

and our exchanges stable. And we are compelled to choose.

In pre-war days, when almost the whole world was on a gold standard, we had all plumped for stability of exchange as against stability of prices, and we were ready to submit to the social consequences of a change of price level for causes quite outside our control, connected, for example, with the discovery of new gold mines in foreign countries or a change of banking policy abroad. But we submitted, partly because we did not dare trust ourselves to a less automatic (though more reasoned) policy, and partly because the price fluctuations experienced were in fact moderate. Nevertheless, there were powerful advocates of the other choice. In particular, the proposals of Professor Irving Fisher for a Compensated Dollar, amounted, unless all countries adopted the same plan, to putting into practice a preference for stability of internal price level over stability of external exchange.

The right choice is not necessarily the same for all countries. It must partly depend on the relative importance of foreign trade in the economic life of the country. Nevertheless, there does seem to be in almost every case a presumption in favour of the stability of prices, if only it can be achieved. Stability of exchange is in the nature of a convenience which adds to the efficiency and prosperity of those who are engaged in foreign trade. Stability of prices,

on the other hand, is profoundly important for the
avoidance of the various evils described in Chapter I.
Contracts and business expectations, which presume
a stable exchange, must be far fewer, even in a
trading country such as England, than those which
presume a stable level of internal prices. The main
argument to the contrary seems to be that exchange
stability is an easier aim to attain, since it only
requires that the same standard of value should be
adopted at home and abroad ; whereas an internal
standard, so regulated as to maintain stability in an
index number of prices, is a difficult scientific innovation, never yet put into practice.

There has been an interesting example recently of
a country which, more perhaps by chance than by
design, has secured the advantages of a relatively stable
level of internal prices at the expense of a fluctuating
exchange, namely India. Public attention is so
much fixed on the exchange as the test of the success
of a financial policy, that the Government of India,
under severe reproaches for what has happened,
have not defended themselves as effectively as they
might. During the boom of 1919–20, when world
prices were soaring, the exchange value of the rupee
was allowed to rise by successive stages, with the result
that the highest level reached by the Indian index
number in 1920 exceeded by only 12 per cent the
average figure for 1919, whereas for England the figure
was 29 per cent. The Report of the Indian Currency

Committee, on which the Government of India acted somewhat clumsily without enough allowance for rapidly changing conditions, was avowedly influenced by the importance in such a country as India, especially in the political circumstances of that time, of avoiding a violent upward movement of internal prices. The most just criticism of the Government of India's action, in the light of after-events, is that they went too far in attempting to raise the rupee so high as 2s. 8d.,—a rate not contemplated by the Currency Committee. Prices outside India never rose so high as to justify an exchange exceeding 2s. 3d. on the criterion of keeping Indian prices stable at the 1919 level. On the other hand, when world prices collapsed, the rupee exchange was allowed to fall with them, again with the result that the lowest point touched by the Indian index number in 1921 was only 16 per cent below the highest in 1920, whereas for England the figure was 50 per cent. The following table gives the details :

	Indian Prices.	English Prices.[1]	Value of Rupee in Sterling.	
			Purchasing Power Parity.	Actual Exchange.
Average 1919	100	100	100	100
Highest 1920	112	129	115	152
Lowest 1921	95	65	69	72
Average 1922	90	64	71	74

[1] *Statist.*

If the Government of India had been successful in stabilising the rupee-sterling exchange, they would necessarily have subjected India to a disastrous price fluctuation comparable to that in England. Thus the unthinking assumption, in favour of the restoration of a fixed exchange as the one thing to aim at, requires more examination than it sometimes receives.

Especially is this the case if the prospect that a majority of countries will adopt the same standard is still remote. When by adopting the gold standard we could achieve stability of exchange with almost the whole world, whilst any other standard would have appeared as a solitary eccentricity, the solid advantages of certainty and convenience supported the conservative preference for gold. Nevertheless, even so, the convenience of traders and the primitive passion for solid metal might not, I think, have been adequate to preserve the dynasty of gold, if it had not been for another, half-accidental circumstance ; namely, that for many years past gold had afforded not only a stable exchange but, on the whole, a stable price level also. In fact, the choice between stable exchanges and stable prices had not presented itself as an acute dilemma. And when, prior to the development of the South African mines, we seemed to be faced with a continuously falling price level, the fierceness of the bimetallic controversy testified to the discontent provoked as soon as the existing standard appeared seriously incompatible with the stability of prices.

Indeed, it is doubtful whether the pre-war system for regulating the international flow of gold would have been capable of dealing with such large or sudden divergencies between the price levels of different countries as have occurred lately. The fault of the pre-war régime, under which the rates of exchange between a country and the outside world were fixed, and the internal price level had to adjust itself thereto (*i.e.* was chiefly governed by external influences), was that it was too slow and insensitive in its mode of operation. The fault of the post-war régime, under which the price level mainly depends on internal influences (*i.e.* internal currency and credit policy) and the rates of exchange with the outside world have to adjust themselves thereto, is that it is too rapid in its effect and over-sensitive, with the result that it may act violently for merely transitory causes. Nevertheless, when the fluctuations are large and sudden, a quick reaction is necessary for the maintenance of equilibrium ; and the necessity for quick reaction has been one of the factors which have rendered the pre-war method inapplicable to post-war conditions, and have made every one nervous of proclaiming a final fixation of the exchange.

We are familiar with the causal chain along which the pre-war method reached its result. If gold flowed out of the country's central reserves, this modified discount policy and the creation of credit, thus affecting the demand for, and hence the price of, the class of goods most sensitive to the ease of credit, and gradually, through the price of these goods, spreading its influence to the prices of goods generally, including those which enter into international trade, until at the new level of price foreign goods began to look dear at home and domestic goods cheap abroad, and the adverse balance was redressed. But this process might take months to work itself out. Nowadays, the gold reserves might be dangerously depleted before the compensating forces had time to operate. Moreover, the movement of the rate of interest up or down sometimes had more effect in attracting foreign capital or encouraging investment abroad than in influencing home prices. Where the disequilibrium was purely seasonal, this was an unqualified advantage; for it was much better that foreign funds should ebb and flow between the slack and the busy seasons than that prices should go up and down. But where it was due to more permanent causes, the adjustment even before the war might be imperfect; for the stimulus to foreign loans, whilst restoring the balance for the time being, might obscure the real seriousness of the situation, and enable a country to live beyond its resources for a considerable time at the risk of ultimate default.

Compare with this the instantaneous effects of the post-war method. If at the existing rate of exchange the amount of sterling offered in the exchange market during the course of the morning exceeds the amount of dollars offered, there is no gold available for export at a fixed price to bridge the gulf. Consequently the dollar rate of exchange must move until at the new rate the offerings of each of the two currencies in exchange for one another exactly balance in amount. But it is the inevitable result of this that within half an hour the relative prices of commodities entering into English-American trade, such as cotton and electrolytic copper, have adjusted themselves accordingly. Unless the American prices move to meet them half-way, the English prices immediately rise correspondent to the movement of the exchange.

This means that relative prices can be knocked about by the most fleeting influences of politics and of sentiment, and by the periodic pressure of seasonal trades. But it also means that the post-war method is a most rapid and powerful corrective of real disequilibria in the balance of international payments arising from whatever causes, and a wonderful preventive in the way of countries which are inclined to spend abroad beyond their resources.

Thus when there are violent shocks to the preexisting equilibrium between the internal and external price-levels, the pre-war method is likely to break down in practice, simply because it cannot bring about the re-adjustment of internal prices *quick enough*. Theoretically, of course, the pre-war method must

be able to make itself effective sooner or later, provided the movement of gold is allowed to continue
without restriction, until the inflation or deflation
of prices has taken place to the necessary extent.
But in practice there is usually a limit to the rate
and to the amount by which the actual currency or
the metallic backing for it can be allowed to flow
abroad.   If the supply of money or credit is reduced
faster than social and business arrangements allow
prices to fall, intolerable inconveniences result.
Perhaps some of the incidents of debasement of the
coinage which are sprinkled through the currency
history of the late Middle Ages were really due to
a similar cause.   Prior to the discovery of the New
World the precious metals were, over a long period,
becoming progressively scarcer in Europe through
natural wastage in the absence of adequate new
supplies, and the drain to the East ; with the result
that from time to time the price level in England
(for example) would be established on too high a
level in relation to European prices.   The resulting
tendency of silver to flow abroad, being accentuated
perhaps by some special temporary cause, would
give rise to complaints of a " scarcity of currency,"
which really means an outflow of money faster
than social organisation permits prices to fall.   No
doubt some of the debasements were helped by
the fact that they profited incidentally a necessitous
Exchequer.   But they may have been, nevertheless,

the best available expedient for meeting the currency problem.[1] We shall look on Edward III.'s debasements of sterling money with a more tolerant eye if we regard them as a method of carrying into effect a preference for stability of internal prices over stability of external exchanges, celebrating that monarch as an enlightened forerunner of Professor Irving Fisher in advocacy of the " compensated dollar," only more happy than the latter in his opportunities to carry theory into practice.

The reader should notice, further, the different parts played by discount policy under the one régime and under the other. With the pre-war method discount policy is a vital part of the process for restoring equilibrium between internal and external prices. With the post-war method it is not equally indispensable, since the fluctuation of the exchanges can bring about equilibrium without its aid ;— though it remains, of course, as an instrument for influencing the internal price level and through this the exchanges, if we desire to establish either the one or the other at a different level from that which would have prevailed otherwise.

III. *The Restoration of a Gold Standard.*

Our conclusions up to this point are, therefore, that, when stability of the internal price level and stability of the external exchanges are incompatible,

---

[1] Cf. Hawtrey, *Currency and Credit*, chap. xvii.

the former is generally preferable ; and that on occasions when the dilemma is acute, the preservation of the former at the expense of the latter is, fortunately perhaps, the line of least resistance.

The restoration of the gold standard (whether at the pre-war parity or at some other rate) certainly will not give us complete stability of internal prices and can only give us complete stability of the external exchanges if all other countries also restore the gold standard. The advisability of restoring it depends, therefore, on whether, on the whole, it will give us the best working compromise obtainable between the two ideals.

The advocates of gold, as against a more scientific standard, base their cause on the double contention, that in practice gold has provided and will provide a reasonably stable standard of value, and that in practice, since governing authorities lack wisdom as often as not, a managed currency will, sooner or later, come to grief. Conservatism and scepticism join arms—as they often do. Perhaps superstition comes in too ; for gold still enjoys the prestige of its smell and colour.

The considerable success with which gold maintained its stability of value in the changing world of the nineteenth century was certainly remarkable. I have applauded it in the first chapter. After the discoveries of Australia and California it began to depreciate dangerously, and before the exploitation of South Africa it began to appreciate dangerously. Yet in each case it righted itself and retained its reputation.

But the conditions of the future are not those of the past. We have no sufficient ground for expecting the continuance of the special conditions which preserved a sort of balance before the war. For what are the underlying explanations of the good behaviour of gold during the nineteenth century?

In the first place, it happened that progress in the discovery of gold mines roughly kept pace with progress in other directions—a correspondence which was not altogether a matter of chance, because the progress of that period, since it was characterised by the gradual opening up and exploitation of the world's surface, not unnaturally brought to light *pari passu* the remoter deposits of gold. But this stage of history is now almost at an end. A quarter of a century has passed by since the discovery of an important deposit. Material progress is more dependent now on the growth of scientific and technical knowledge, of which the application to gold-mining may be intermittent. Years may elapse without great improvement in the methods of extracting gold; and then the genius of a chemist may realise past dreams and forgotten hoaxes, transmuting base into precious like Subtle, or extracting gold from sea-water as in the Bubble. Gold is liable to be either too dear or too cheap. In either case, it is too much to expect that a succession of accidents will keep the metal steady.

But there was another type of influence which used to aid stability. The value of gold has not depended on the policy or the decisions of a single body of men; and a sufficient proportion of the supply has been able to find its way, without any flooding of the market, into the Arts or into the hoards of Asia for its marginal value to be governed by a steady psychological estimation of the metal in relation to other things. This is what is meant by saying that gold has " intrinsic value " and is free from the dangers of a " managed " currency. The *independent variety* of the influences determining the value of gold has been in itself a steadying influence. The arbitrary and variable character of the proportion of gold reserves to liabilities maintained by many of the note-issuing banks of the world, so far from introducing an incalculable factor, was an element of stability. For when gold was relatively abundant and flowed towards them, it was absorbed by their allowing their ratio of gold reserves to rise slightly; and when it was relatively scarce, the fact that they had no intention of ever utilising their gold reserves for any practical purpose, permitted most of them to view with equanimity a moderate weakening of their proportion. A great part of the flow of South African gold between the end of the Boer War and 1914 was able to find its way into the central gold reserves of European and other countries with the minimum effect on prices.

But the war has effected a great change. Gold itself has become a " managed " currency. The West, as well as the East, has learnt to hoard gold ; but the motives of the United States are not those of India. Now that most countries have abandoned the gold standard, the supply of the metal would, if the chief user of it restricted its holdings to its real needs, prove largely redundant. The United States has not been able to let gold fall to its " natural " value, because it could not face the resulting depreciation of its standard. It has been driven, therefore, to the costly policy of burying in the vaults of Washington what the miners of the Rand have laboriously brought to the surface. Consequently gold now stands at an " artificial " value, the future course of which almost entirely depends on the policy of the Federal Reserve Board of the United States. The value of gold is no longer the resultant of the chance gifts of Nature and the judgment of numerous authorities and individuals acting independently. Even if other countries gradually return to a gold basis, the position will not be greatly changed. The tendency to employ some variant of the gold-exchange standard and the probably permanent disappearance of gold from the pockets of the people are likely to mean that the strictly *necessary* gold reserves of the Central Banks of the gold-standard countries will fall considerably short of the available supplies. The actual value of gold will depend, therefore, on the policy of three or four of the most powerful Central Banks, whether they act independently or in unison. If, on the other hand, pre-war conventions about the use of gold in reserves and in circulation were to be restored—which is, in my opinion, the much less probable alternative—there might be, as Professor Cassel has predicted, a serious shortage of gold leading to a progressive appreciation in its value.

Nor must we neglect the possibility of a partial demonetisation of gold by the United States through a closing of its mints to further receipts of gold. The present policy of the United States in accepting unlimited imports of gold can be justified, perhaps, as a temporary measure, intended to preserve tradition and to strengthen confidence through a transitional period. But, looked at as a permanent arrangement, it could hardly be judged otherwise than as a foolish expense. If the Federal Reserve Board intends to maintain the value of the dollar at a level which is irrespective of the inflow or outflow of gold, what object is there in continuing to accept at the mints gold which is not wanted, yet costs a heavy price ? If the United States mints were to be closed to gold, everything, except the actual price of the metal, could continue precisely as before.

Confidence in the future stability of the value of gold depends therefore on the United States being foolish enough to go on accepting gold which it does not want, and wise enough, having accepted it, to maintain it at a fixed value. This double event might be realised through the collaboration of a public understanding nothing with a Federal Reserve Board understanding everything. But the position is precarious ; and not very attractive to any country which is still in a position to choose what its future standard is to be.

This discussion of the prospects of the stability of gold has partly answered by anticipation the second principal argument in favour of the restoration of an unqualified gold standard, namely that this is the only way of avoiding the dangers of a " managed " currency.

It is natural, after what we have experienced, that prudent people should desiderate a standard of value which is independent of Finance Ministers and State Banks. The present state of affairs has allowed to the ignorance and frivolity of statesmen an ample opportunity of bringing about ruinous consequences in the economic field. It is felt that the general level of economic and financial education amongst statesmen and bankers is hardly such as to render innovations feasible or safe ; that, in fact, a chief object of stabilising the exchanges is to strap down Ministers of Finance.

These are reasonable grounds of hesitation. But the experience on which they are based is by no means fair to the capacities of statesmen and bankers. The non-metallic standards, of which we have experience, have been anything rather than scientific experiments coolly carried out. They have been a last resort, involuntarily adopted, as a result of war or inflationary taxation, when the State finances were already broken or the situation out of hand. Naturally in these circumstances such practices have been the accompaniment and the prelude of disaster. But we cannot argue from this to what can be achieved in normal times. I do not see that the regulation of the standard of value is essentially more difficult than many other objects of less social necessity which we attain successfully.

If, indeed, a providence watched over gold, or if Nature had provided us with a stable standard ready-made, I would not, in an attempt after some slight improvement, hand over the management to the possible weakness or ignorance of Boards and Governments. But this is not the situation. We have no ready-made standard. Experience has shown that in emergencies Ministers of Finance cannot be strapped down. And—most important of all—in the modern world of paper currency and bank credit there is no escape from a " managed " currency, whether we wish it or not ;—convertibility into gold will not alter the fact that the value of gold itself depends on the policy of the Central Banks.

It is worth while to pause a moment over the last

sentence. It differs significantly from the doctrine
of gold reserves which we learnt and taught before
the war. We used to assume that no Central Bank
would be so extravagant as to keep more gold than
it required or so imprudent as to keep less. From
time to time gold would flow out into the circulation
or for export abroad ; experience showed that the
quantity required on these occasions bore some rough
proportion to the Central Bank's liabilities ; a
decidedly higher proportion than this would be fixed
on to provide for contingencies and to inspire confidence ; and the creation of credit would be regulated
largely by reference to the maintenance of this
proportion. The Bank of England, for example,
would allow itself to be swayed by the tides of gold,
permitting the inflowing and outflowing streams to
produce their " natural " consequences unchecked by
any ideas as to preventing the effect on prices.
Already before the war, the system was becoming
precarious by reason of its artificiality. The " proportion " was by the lapse of time losing its relation
to the facts and had become largely conventional.
Some other figure, greater or less, would have done
just as well.[1] The War broke down the convention ;
for the withdrawal of gold from actual circulation
destroyed one of the elements of reality lying behind
the convention, and the suspension of convertibility

---

[1] *Vide,* for what I wrote about this in 1914, *The Economic Journal,*
xxiv. p. 621.

destroyed the other.   It would have been absurd to regulate the bank rate by reference to a " proportion " which had lost all its significance ; and in the course of the past ten years a new policy has been evolved. The bank rate is now employed, however incompletely and experimentally, to regulate the expansion and deflation of credit in the interests of business stability and the steadiness of prices.   In so far as it is employed to procure stability of the dollar exchange, where this is inconsistent with stability of internal prices, we have a relic of pre-war policy and a compromise between discrepant aims.

Those who advocate the return to a gold standard do not always appreciate along what different lines our actual practice has been drifting.   If we restore the gold standard, are we to return also to the pre-war conceptions of bank-rate, allowing the tides of gold to play what tricks they like with the internal price-level, and abandoning the attempt to moderate the disastrous influence of the credit-cycle on the stability of prices and employment ?   Or are we to continue and develop the experimental innovations of our present policy, ignoring the " bank ratio " and, if necessary, allowing unmoved a piling up of gold reserves far beyond our requirements or their depletion far below them ?

In truth, the gold standard is already a barbarous relic.   All of us, from the Governor of the Bank of England downwards, are now primarily interested in preserving the stability of business, prices, and employment, and are not likely, when the choice is forced on us, deliberately to sacrifice these to the outworn dogma, which had its value once, of £3 : 17 : 10½ per ounce. Advocates of the ancient standard do not observe how remote it now is from the spirit and the requirements of the age. A regulated non-metallic standard has slipped in unnoticed. *It exists.* Whilst the economists dozed, the academic dream of a hundred years, doffing its cap and gown, clad in paper rags, has crept into the real world by means of the bad fairies—always so much more potent than the good—the wicked Ministers of Finance.

For these reasons enlightened advocates of the restoration of gold, such as Mr. Hawtrey, do not welcome it as the return of a "natural" currency, and intend, quite decidedly, that it shall be a "managed" one. They allow gold back only as a constitutional monarch, shorn of his ancient despotic powers and compelled to accept the advice of a Parliament of Banks. The adoption of the ideas present in the minds of those who drafted the Genoa Resolutions on Currency is an essential condition of Mr. Hawtrey's adherence to gold. He contemplates "the practice of continuous co-operation among central banks of issue" (Res. 3), and an international convention, based on a gold exchange standard, and designed "with a view to preventing undue fluctuations in the purchasing power of gold " (Res. 11).[1] But he is *not* in favour of resuming the gold standard irrespective of " whether the difficulties in regard to the future purchasing power of gold have been provided against or not." " It is not easy," he admits, " to promote international action, and should it fail, the wisest course for the time being might be to concentrate on the stabilisation of sterling in terms of commodities, rather than tie the pound to a metal, the vagaries of which cannot be foreseen." [2]

It is natural to ask, in face of advocacy of this kind, why it is necessary to drag in gold at all. Mr. Hawtrey lays no stress on the obvious support for his compromise, namely the force of sentiment and tradition, and the preference of Englishmen for shearing a monarch of his powers rather than of his head. But he adduces three other reasons : (1) that gold is required as a liquid reserve for the settlement of international balances of indebtedness ; (2) that it enables an experiment to be made without cutting adrift from the old system ; and (3) that the vested interests of gold producers must be considered. These objects, however, are so largely attained by my own suggestions in the following chapter, that I need not dwell on them here.

On the other hand, I see grave objections to reinstating gold in the pious hope that international co-operation will keep it in order. With the existing

[1] *Monetary Reconstruction*, p. 132.   [2] *Loc. cit.* p. 22.

distribution of the world's gold, the reinstatement of the gold standard means, inevitably, that we surrender the regulation of our price level and the handling of the credit cycle to the Federal Reserve Board of the United States.   Even if the most intimate and cordial co-operation is established between the Board and the Bank of England, the preponderance of power will still belong to the former.   The Board will be in a position to disregard the Bank.   But if the Bank disregard the Board, it will render itself liable to be flooded with, or depleted of, gold, as the case may be. Moreover, we can be confident beforehand that there will be much suspicion amongst Americans (for that is their disposition) of any supposed attempt on the part of the Bank of England to dictate their policy or to influence American discount rates in the interests of Great Britain.   We must also be prepared to incur our share of the vain expense of bottling up the world's redundant gold.

It would be rash in present circumstances to surrender our freedom of action to the Federal Reserve Board of the United States.   We do not yet possess sufficient experience of its capacity to act in times of stress with courage and independence.   The Federal Reserve Board is striving to free itself from the pressure of sectional interests ; but we are not yet certain that it will wholly succeed.   It is still liable to be overwhelmed by the impetuosity of a cheap money campaign.   A suspicion of British influence would, so far from strengthening the Board, greatly weaken its resistance to popular clamour. Nor is it certain, quite apart from weakness or mistakes, that the simultaneous application of the same policy will always be in the interests of both countries. The development of the credit cycle and the state of business may sometimes be widely different on the two sides of the Atlantic.

Therefore, since I regard the stability of prices, credit, and employment as of paramount importance, and since I feel no confidence that an old-fashioned gold standard will even give us the modicum of stability that it used to give, I reject the policy of restoring the gold standard on pre-war lines. At the same time I doubt the wisdom of attempting a " managed " gold standard jointly with the United States, on the lines recommended by Mr. Hawtrey, because it retains too many of the disadvantages of the old system without its advantages, and because it would make us too dependent on the policy and on the wishes of the Federal Reserve Board.

CHAPTER V

A SOUND constructive scheme must provide—if it is to satisfy the arguments and the analysis of this book :

I. A method for regulating the supply of currency and credit with a view to maintaining, so far as possible, the stability of the internal price level ; and

II. A method for regulating the supply of foreign exchange so as to avoid purely temporary fluctuations, caused by seasonal or other influences and not due to a lasting disturbance in the relation between the internal and the external price level.

I believe that in Great Britain the ideal system can be most nearly and most easily reached by an adaptation of the actual system which has grown up, half haphazard, since the war. After the general idea has been exhibited by an application in detail to the case of Great Britain, it will be sufficient to deal somewhat briefly with the modifications required in the case of other countries.

I. *Great Britain.*

The system actually in operation to-day is broadly as follows :

(1) The internal price level is mainly determined by the amount of credit created by the banks, chiefly the Big Five ; though in a depression, when the public are increasing their real balances, a greater amount of credit has to be created to support a given price level (in accordance with the theory explained above in Chapter III., p. 84) than is required in a boom, when real balances are being diminished.

The amount of credit, so created, is in its turn roughly measured by the volume of the banks' deposits—since variations in this total must correspond to variations in the total of their investments, bill-holdings, and advances. Now there is no necessary reason *a priori* why the proportion between the banks' deposits and their " cash in hand and at the Bank of England " should not fluctuate within fairly wide limits in accordance with circumstances. But in practice the banks usually work by rule of thumb and do not depart widely from their preconceived " proportions." [1] In recent times their aggregate

---

[1] The Joint Stock banks have published monthly returns since January 1921. Excluding the half-yearly statement when a little " window-dressing" is temporarily arranged, the extreme range of fluctuation has been between 11·0 per cent and 11·9 per cent in the proportion of " cash " to deposits, and between 41·1 per cent and 50·1 per cent in the proportion of advances to deposits. These figures cover two and a half years of widely varying conditions. The " proportions " of individual banks differ amongst themselves, and the above is an average result, the steadiness of which is strengthened by the fact that each big bank is pretty steadfast in its own policy.

deposits have always been about nine times their
" cash." Since this is what is generally considered a
" safe " proportion, it is bad for a bank's reputation
to fall below it, whilst on the other hand it is bad for
its earning power to rise above it. Thus in one way
or another the banks generally adjust their total
creation of credit in one form or another (investments, bills, and advances) up to their capacity as
measured by the above criterion ; from which it
follows that the volume of their " cash " in the shape
of Bank and Currency Notes and Deposits at the
Bank of England closely determines the volume of
credit which they create.

In order to follow, therefore, the train of causation
a stage further, we must consider what determines
the volume of their " cash." Its amount can only
be altered in one or other of three ways : (*a*) by the
public requiring more or fewer notes in circulation,
(*b*) by the Treasury borrowing more or less from the
Currency Note Reserve, and (*c*) by the Bank of
England increasing or diminishing its assets.[1]

To complete the argument, one further factor, not
yet mentioned, must be introduced, namely (*d*) the
proportion of the banks' second-line reserve in the
shape of their holdings of Treasury Bills, which can
be regarded as cash at one remove. In determining
what is a safe proportion of " cash," they pay some

---

[1] For the aggregate of its liabilities in the shape of deposits and of notes
in circulation automatically depends on the volume of its assets.

regard to the amount of Treasury Bills which they hold, since by reducing this holding they can immediately increase their " cash " and compel the Treasury to borrow more either from the Currency Note Reserve or from the Bank of England. The ninefold proportion referred to above presumes a certain minimum holding of Treasury Bills, and might have to be modified if a sufficient volume of such Bills was not available. This factor (d) is, however, also important because the banks in their turn are open to pressure by the Treasury, whenever it draws to itself the resources of their depositors— whether by taxation or by offering them attractive longer-dated loans—and uses them to pay off, if not Ways and Means advances from the Bank of England (which reduces the banks' first-line reserve of cash), then alternatively Treasury Bills held by the banks themselves (which reduces their second-line reserve of bills).

Items (a), (b), (c), and (d) together, therefore, more or less settle the matter. For the purpose of the present argument, however, we need not pay much separate attention to (a) and (b), since their effect is, for the most part, reflected over again in (c) and (d). (a) depends partly on the volume of trade but mainly on the price level itself ; and in practice fluctuations in (a) do not *directly* affect the banks' " cash,"—for if more notes are required under (a), more notes are issued, the Treasury borrowing a corresponding additional amount from the Currency Note Reserve, in which case the Treasury either repays the Bank of England, which diminishes the Bank's assets and consequently the other banks' " cash," or withdraws an equivalent amount of Treasury Bills, which diminishes the other banks' second-line reserve ; *i.e.* a change in (*a*) operates on the banks' resources through (*c*) and (*d*).[1] Whilst as for (*b*), a change in the amount of what the Treasury borrows from the Currency Note Reserve is reflected by a corresponding change in the opposite sense in what it borrows in Ways and Means Advances or in Treasury Bills.

Thus we can concentrate our attention on (*c*) and (*d*) as the main determining factors of the price level.

Now (*c*), namely the assets of the Bank of England, consist (so far as their variable part is concerned) of

(i.) Ways and Means advances to the Treasury.

(ii.) Gilt-edged and other investments.

(iii.) Advances to its customers and bills of exchange.

(iv.) Gold.

An increase in any of these items tends, therefore, to increase the other banks' " cash," thereby to stimulate the creation of credit, and hence to raise the price level ; and contrariwise.

And (*d*), namely the banks' holdings of Treasury Bills, depend on the excess of the expenditure of the

[1] If the additional issue of notes is covered by transferring gold from the Bank of England, this is merely an alternative way of diminishing the Bank of England's assets.

Treasury over and above what it secures (i.) from the public by taxation and loans, (ii.) from the Bank of England in Ways and Means advances, and (iii.) by borrowing from the Currency Note Reserve.

It follows that the capacity of the Joint Stock banks to create credit is mainly governed by the policies and actions of the Bank of England and of the Treasury. When these are settled, (*a*), (*b*), (*c*), and (*d*) are settled.

How far can these two authorities control their own actions and how far must they remain passive agents ? In my opinion the control, if they choose to exercise it, is mainly in their own hands. As regards the Treasury, the extent to which they draw money from the public to discharge floating debt clearly depends on the rate of interest and the type of loan which they are prepared to offer. A point might be reached when they could not fund further on any reasonable terms; but within fairly wide limits the policy of the Treasury can be whatever the Chancellor of the Exchequer and the House of Commons may decide. The Bank of England also is, within sufficiently wide limits, mistress of the situation if she acts in conjunction with the Treasury. She can increase or decrease at will her investments and her gold by buying or selling the one or the other. In the case of advances and of bills, whilst their volume is not so immediately or directly control-lable, here also adequate control can be obtained

by varying the price charged, that is to say the bank
rate.[1]

Therefore it is broadly true to say that the level
of prices, and hence the level of the exchanges,
depends in the last resort on the policy of the Bank
of England and of the Treasury in respect of the above
particulars ;—though the other banks, if they strongly
opposed the official policy, could thwart, or at least
delay it to a certain extent—provided they were
prepared to depart from their usual proportions.

(2) Cash, in the form of Bank or Currency Notes,
is supplied *ad libitum, i.e.* in such quantities as are
called for by the amount of credit created and the
internal price level established under (1). That is
to say, in practice ;—in theory, a limit to the issue
of Currency Notes has been laid down, namely the
maximum fiduciary issue actually attained in the
preceding calendar year. Since this theoretical maximum was prescribed, it has never yet been actually

[1] It is often assumed that the bank rate is the *sole* governing factor.
But the bank rate can only operate by its reaction on (c), namely, the Bank
of England's assets.   Formerly it acted pretty directly on two of the components of (c), namely, (c) (iii.) advances to customers and bills of exchange
and (c) (iv.) gold.   Now it acts only on one of them, namely, (c) (iii.).   But
changes in (c) (i.) the Bank's advances to the Treasury and (c) (ii.) the Bank's
investments can often be nearly as potent in their effect on the creation of
credit.   Thus a low bank rate can be largely neutralised by a simultaneous
reduction of (c) (i.) or (c) (ii.) and a high bank rate by an increase of these.
Indeed the Bank of England can probably bring the money-market to heel
more decisively by buying or selling securities than in any other way ;
and the utility of bank rate, operated by itself and without assistance from
deliberate variations in the volume of (c) (ii.), is lessened by the various
limitations which exist in practice to its freedom of movement, and to the
limits within which it can move, upwards and downwards.

operative ; and, as the rule springs from a doctrine now out of date and out of accordance with most responsible opinion, it is probable that, if it were becoming operative, it would be relaxed. This is a matter where the recommendations of the Cunliffe Committee call for urgent change, unless we desire deliberately to pursue still further a process of Deflation. A point must come when, a year of brisk trade and employment following one of depression, there will be an increased demand for currency, which must be met unless the revival is to be deliberately damped down.

Thus the tendency of to-day—rightly I think— is to watch and to control the creation of credit and to let the creation of currency follow suit, rather than, as formerly, to watch and to control the creation of currency and to let the creation of credit follow suit.

(3) The Bank of England's gold is immobilised. It neither buys nor sells. The gold plays no part in our system. Occasionally, however, the Bank may ship a consignment to the United States, to help the Treasury in meeting its dollar liabilities. The South African and other gold which finds its way here comes purely as a commodity to a convenient *entrepôt* centre, and is mostly re-exported.

(4) The foreign exchanges are unregulated and left to look after themselves. From day to day they fluctuate in accordance with the seasons and other irregular influences. Over longer periods they

depend, as we have seen, on the relative price levels established here and abroad by the respective credit policies adopted here and abroad. But whilst this is, for the most part, the actual state of affairs, it is not, as yet, the avowed or consistent policy of the responsible authorities. Fixity of the dollar exchange at the pre-war parity remains their aspiration ; and it still may happen that the bank rate is raised for the purpose of influencing the exchange at a time when considerations of internal price level and credit policy point the other way.

This, in brief—I apologise to the reader if I have compressed the argument unduly — is the present state of affairs, one essentially different from our pre-war system. It will be observed that in practice we have already gone a long way towards the ideal of directing bank rate and credit policy by reference to the internal price level and other symptoms of under- or over-expansion of internal credit, rather than by reference to the pre-war criteria of the amount of cash in circulation (or of gold reserves in the banks) or the level of the dollar exchange.

I. Accordingly my first requirement in a good constructive scheme can be supplied merely by a development of our existing arrangements on more deliberate and self-conscious lines. Hitherto the Treasury and the Bank of England have looked forward to the stability of the dollar exchange (preferably at the pre-war parity) as their objective. It is not clear whether they intend to stick to this irrespective of fluctuations in the value of the dollar (or of gold); whether, that is to say, they would sacrifice the stability of sterling prices to the stability of the dollar exchange in the event of the two proving to be incompatible. At any rate, my scheme would require that they should adopt the stability of sterling prices as their *primary* objective—though this would not prevent their aiming at exchange stability also as a secondary objective by co-operating with the Federal Reserve Board in a common policy. So long as the Federal Reserve Board was successful in keeping dollar prices steady the objective of keeping sterling prices steady would be identical with the objective of keeping the dollar sterling exchange steady. My recommendation does not involve more than a determination that, in the event of the Federal Reserve Board failing to keep dollar prices steady, sterling prices should not, if it could be helped, plunge with them merely for the sake of maintaining a fixed parity of exchange.

If the Bank of England, the Treasury, and the Big Five were to adopt this policy, to what criteria should they look respectively in regulating bank-rate, Government borrowing, and trade-advances? The first question is whether the criterion should be a precise, arithmetical formula or whether it should be sought in a general judgement of the situation based on all the available data. The pioneer of price-stability as against exchange-stability, Professor Irving Fisher, advocated the former in the shape of his " compensated dollar," which was to be auto-matically adjusted by reference to an index number of prices without any play of judgement or discre-tion. He may have been influenced, however, by the advantage of propounding a method which could be grafted as easily as possible on to the pre-war system of gold-reserves and gold-ratios. In any case, I doubt the wisdom and the practicability of a system so cut and dried. If we wait until a price movement is actually afoot before applying remedial measures, we may be too late. " It is not the *past* rise in prices but the *future* rise that has to be counter-acted." [1] It is characteristic of the impetuosity of the credit cycle that price movements tend to be cumulative, each movement promoting, up to a certain point, a further movement in the same direction. Professor Fisher's method may be adapted to deal with long-period trends in the value of gold but not with the, often more injurious, short-period oscillations of the credit cycle. Nevertheless, whilst it would not be advisable to postpone action until it was called for by an actual movement of prices, it would promote confidence and furnish an objective standard of value, if, an official index number having been compiled of such a character as to register the

[1] Hawtrey, *Monetary Reconstruction*, p. 105.

price of a standard composite commodity, the authorities were to adopt this composite commodity as their standard of value in the sense that they would employ all their resources to prevent a movement of its price by more than a certain percentage in either direction away from the normal, just as before the war they employed all their resources to prevent a movement in the price of gold by more than a certain percentage. The precise composition of the standard composite commodity could be modified from time to time in accordance with changes in the relative economic importance of its various components.

As regards the criteria, other than the actual trend of prices, which should determine the action of the controlling authority, it is beyond the scope of this volume to deal adequately with the diagnosis and analysis of the credit cycle. The more deeply that our researches penetrate into this subject, the more accurately shall we understand the right time and method for controlling credit-expansion by bank-rate or otherwise. But in the meantime we have a considerable and growing body of general experience upon which those in authority can base their judgements. Actual price-movements must of course provide the most important datum; but the state of employment, the volume of production, the effective demand for credit as felt by the banks, the rate of interest on investments of various types, the volume of new issues, the flow of cash into circulation, the statistics of foreign trade and the level of the exchanges must all be taken into account. The main point is that the *objective* of the authorities, pursued with such means as are at their command, should be the stability of prices.

It would at least be possible to avoid, for example, such action as has been taken lately (in Great Britain) whereby the supply of " cash " has been deflated at a time when real balances were becoming inflated,— action which has materially aggravated the severity of the late depression.   We might be able to moderate very greatly the amplitude of the fluctuations if it was understood that the time to deflate the supply of cash is when real balances are falling, *i.e.* when prices are rising out of proportion to the increase, if any, in the volume of cash, and that the time to inflate the supply of cash is when real balances are rising, and not, as seems to be our present practice, the other way round.

II. How can we best combine this primary object with a maximum stability of the exchanges ?   Can we get the best of both worlds—stability of prices over long periods and stability of exchanges over short periods ?   It is the great advantage of the gold standard that it overcomes the excessive sensitiveness of the exchanges to temporary influences, which we analysed in Chapter III.   Our object must be to secure this advantage, if we can, without committing ourselves to follow big movements in the value of gold itself.

I believe that we can go a long way in this direction if the Bank of England will take over the duty of regulating the price of gold, just as it already regulates the rate of discount. "Regulate," but not "peg." The Bank of England should have a buying and a selling price for gold, just as it did before the war, and this price might remain unchanged for considerable periods, just as bank-rate does. But it would not be fixed or "pegged" once and for all, any more than bank-rate is fixed. The Bank's rate for gold would be announced every Thursday morning at the same time as its rate for discounting bills, with a difference between its buying and selling rates corresponding to the pre-war margin between £3 : 17 : 10½ per oz. and £3 : 17 : 9 per oz. ; except that, in order to obviate too frequent changes in the rate, the difference might be wider than 1½d. per oz.—say, ½ to 1 per cent. A willingness on the part of the Bank both to buy and to sell gold at rates fixed for the time being would keep the dollar-sterling exchange steady within corresponding limits, so that the exchange rate would not move with every breath of wind but only when the Bank had come to a considered judgement that a change was required for the sake of the stability of sterling prices.

If the bank rate and the gold rate in conjunction were leading to an excessive influx or an excessive efflux of gold, the Bank of England would have to decide whether the flow was due to an internal or to an external movement away from stability. To fix our ideas, let us suppose that gold is flowing outwards. If this seemed to be due to a tendency of sterling to depreciate in terms of commodities, the correct remedy would be to raise the bank rate. If, on the other hand, it was due to a tendency of gold to appreciate in terms of commodities, the correct remedy would be to raise the gold rate (*i.e.* the buying price for gold). If, however, the flow could be explained by seasonal, or other passing influences, then it should be allowed to continue (assuming, of course, that the Bank's gold reserves were equal to any probable calls on them) unchecked, to be redressed later on by the corresponding reaction.

Two subsidiary suggestions may be made for strengthening the Bank's control :

(1) The service of the American debt will make it necessary for the British Treasury to buy nearly $500,000 every working day. It is clear that the particular method adopted for purchasing these huge sums will greatly affect the short-period fluctuations of the exchange. I suggest that this duty should be entrusted to the Bank of England to be carried out by them with the express object of minimising those fluctuations in the exchange which are due to the daily and seasonal ebb and flow of the ordinary trade demand. In particular the proper distribution

of these purchases through the year might be so arranged as greatly to mitigate the normal seasonal fluctuation discussed in Chapter III. If the trade demand is concentrated in one half of the year the Treasury demand should be concentrated in the other half.

(2) It would effect an improvement in the technique of the system here proposed, without altering its fundamental characteristics, if the Bank of England were to quote a daily price, not only for the purchase and sale of gold for immediate delivery, but also for delivery three months forward. The difference, if any, between the cash and forward quotations might represent either a discount or a premium of the latter on the former, according as the bank desired money rates in London to stand below or above those in New York. The existence of the forward quotation of the Bank of England would afford a firm foundation for a free market in forward exchange, and would facilitate the movement of funds between London and New York for short periods, in much the same way as before the war, whilst at the same time keeping down to a minimum the actual movement of gold bullion backwards and forwards. I need not develop this point further, because it is only an application of the argument of Section III. of Chapter III. which will be most readily intelligible to the reader, if he will refer back to the previous argument.

There remains the question of the regulation of the Note Issue. My proposal here may appear shocking until the reader realises that, apart from its disregarding the conventions, it does not differ in substance from the existing state of affairs. The object of fixing the amount of gold to be held against a note issue is to set up a danger signal which cannot be easily disregarded, when a curtailment of credit and purchasing power is urgently required to maintain the legal tender money at its lawful parity. But this system, whilst far better than no system at all, is primitive in its ideas and is, in fact, a survival of an earlier evolutionary stage in the development of credit and currency. For it has two great disadvantages. In so far as we fix a minimum gold reserve against the note issue, the effect is to immobilise this quantity of gold and thus to reduce the amount actually available for use as a store of value to meet temporary or sudden deficits in the country's international balance of payments. And in so far as we regard an approach towards the prescribed minimum or a departure upwards from it as a barometer warning us to curtail credit or encouraging us to expand it, we are using a criterion which most people would now agree in considering second-rate for the purpose, because it cannot give the necessary warning *soon enough*. If gold movements are actually taking place, this means that the disequilibrium has proceeded a very long way ; and whilst this criterion may pull us up in time to preserve convertibility on the one hand or to prevent an excessive flood of gold on the other, it will not do so in time to avoid an injurious oscillation of prices. This method belongs indeed to a period when the preservation of convertibility was all that any one thought about (all indeed that there was to think about so long as we were confined to an unregulated gold standard), and before the idea of utilising bank-rate as a means of keeping prices and employment steady had become practical politics.

We have scarcely realised how far our thoughts have travelled during the past five years. But to re-read the famous Cunliffe Report on Currency and Foreign Exchange after the War, published in 1918, brings vividly before one's mind what a great distance we have covered since then. This document was published three months before the Armistice. It was compiled long before the unpegging of sterling and the great break in the European exchanges in 1919, before the tremendous boom and crash of 1920–21, before the vast piling up of the world's gold in America, and without experience of the Federal Reserve policy in 1922–23 of burying this gold at Washington, withdrawing it from the exercise of its full effect on prices, and thereby, in effect, demonetising the metal. The Cunliffe Report is an unadulterated pre-war prescription—inevitably so considering that it was written after four years' interregnum of war, before

Peace was in sight, and without knowledge of the revolutionary and unforeseeable experiences of the past five years.

Of all the omissions from the Cunliffe Report the most noteworthy is the complete absence of any mention of the problem of the stability of the price-level ; and it cheerfully explains how the pre-war system, which it aims at restoring, operated to bring back equilibrium by deliberately causing a " consequent slackening of employment." The Cunliffe Report belongs to an extinct and an almost forgotten order of ideas. Few think on these lines now ; yet the Report remains the authorised declaration of our policy, and the Bank of England and the Treasury are said still to regard it as their marching orders.

Let us return to the regulation of note issue. If we agree that gold is not to be employed in the circulation, and that it is better to employ some other criterion than the ratio of gold reserves to note issue in deciding to raise or to lower the bank rate, it follows that the only employment for gold (nevertheless important) is as a store of value to be held as a war-chest against emergencies and as a means of rapidly correcting the influence of a temporarily adverse balance of international payments and thus maintaining a day-to-day stability of the sterling-dollar exchange. It is desirable, therefore, that the whole of the reserves should be under the control of the authority responsible for this, which, under the above proposals, is the Bank of England. The volume of the paper money, on the other hand, would be consequential, as it is at present, on the state of trade and employment, bank-rate policy and Treasury Bill policy. The governors of the system would be bank-rate and Treasury Bill policy, the objects of government would be stability of trade, prices, and employment, and the volume of paper money would be a consequence of the first (just—I repeat—as it is at present) and an instrument of the second, the precise arithmetical level of which could not and need not be predicted. Nor would the amount of gold, which it would be prudent to hold as a reserve against international emergencies and temporary indebtedness, bear any logical or calculable relation to the volume of paper money;—for the two have no close or necessary connection with one another. Therefore I make the proposal—which may seem, but should not be, shocking—of separating entirely the gold reserve from the note issue. Once this principle is adopted, the regulations are matters of detail. The gold reserves of the country should be concentrated in the hands of the Bank of England, to be used for the purpose of avoiding short-period fluctuations in the exchange. The Currency Notes may, just as well as not—since the Treasury is to draw the profit from them—be issued by the Treasury, without the latter being subjected to any formal regulations (which are likely to be either inoperative or injurious) as to their volume. Except in form, this régime would not differ materially from the existing state of affairs.

The reader will observe that I retain for gold an important rôle in our system. As an ultimate safeguard and as a reserve for sudden requirements, no superior medium is yet available. But I urge that it is possible to get the benefit of the advantages of gold, without irrevocably binding our legal-tender money to follow blindly all the vagaries of gold and future unforeseeable fluctuations in its real purchasing power.

II. *The United States.*

The above proposals are recommended to Great Britain and their details have been adapted to her case. But the principles underlying them remain just as true across the Atlantic. In the United States, as in Great Britain, the methods which are being actually pursued at the present time, half consciously and half unconsciously, are mainly on the lines I advocate. In practice the Federal Reserve Board often ignores the proportion of its gold reserve to its liabilities and is influenced, in determining its discount policy, by the object of maintaining stability in prices, trade, and employment. Out of convention and conservatism it accepts gold. Out of prudence and understanding it buries it. Indeed the theory and investigation of the credit cycle have been taken up so much more enthusiastically and pushed so much further by the economists of the United States than by those of Great Britain, that it would be even more difficult for the Federal Reserve Board than for the Bank of England to ignore such ideas or to avoid being, half-consciously at least, influenced by them.

The theory on which the Federal Reserve Board is supposed to govern its discount policy, by reference to the influx and efflux of gold and the proportion of gold to liabilities, is as dead as mutton. It perished, and perished justly, as soon as the Federal Reserve Board began to ignore its ratio and to accept gold without allowing it to exercise its full influence,[1] merely because an expansion of credit and prices seemed at that moment undesirable. From that day gold was demonetised by almost the last country which still continued to do it lip-service, and a dollar standard was set up on the pedestal of the Golden Calf. For the past two years the United States has *pretended* to maintain a gold standard. *In fact* it has established a dollar standard ; and, instead of ensuring that the value of the dollar shall conform to that of gold, it makes provision, at great expense, that the value of gold shall conform to that of the dollar. This is the way by which a rich

---

[1] The influx of gold could not be prevented from having *some* inflationary effect because its receipt automatically increased the balances of the member banks. This uncontrollable element cannot be avoided so long as the United States Mints are compelled to accept gold. But the gold was not allowed to exercise the multiplied influence which the pre-war system presumed.

country is able to combine new wisdom with old
prejudice. It can enjoy the latest scientific improve-
ments, devised in the economic laboratory of Harvard,
whilst leaving Congress to believe that no rash
departure will be permitted from the hard money
consecrated by the wisdom and experience of Dungi,
Darius, Constantine, Lord Liverpool, and Senator
Aldrich.

No doubt it is worth the expense—for those that
can afford it. The cost of the fiction to the United
States is not more than £100,000,000 per annum and
should not average in the long run above £50,000,000
per annum. But there is in all such fictions a certain
instability. When the accumulations of gold heap
up beyond a certain point the suspicions of Congress-
men may be aroused. One cannot be quite certain
that some Senator might not read and understand
this book. Sooner or later the fiction will lose its
value.

Indeed it is desirable that this should be so. The
new methods will work more efficiently and more
economically when they can be pursued consciously,
deliberately, and openly. The economists of Harvard
know more than those of Washington, and it will be
well that in due course their surreptitious victory
should swell into public triumph. At any rate those
who are responsible for establishing the principles of
British currency should not overlook the possibility
that some day soon the Mints of the United States

may be closed to the acceptance of gold at a fixed dollar price.

Closing the Mints to the compulsory acceptance of gold need not affect the existing obligation of convertibility ;—the liability to encash notes in gold might still remain. Theoretically this might be regarded as a blemish on the perfection of the scheme. But, for the present at least, it is unlikely that such a provision would compel the United States to deflate,—which possibility is the only theoretical objection to it. On the other hand, the retention of convertibility would remain a safeguard satisfactory to old-fashioned people ; and would reduce to a minimum the new and controversial legislation required to effect the change. Many people might agree to relieve the Mint of the liability to accept gold which no one wants, who would be dismayed at any tampering with convertibility. Moreover, in certain quite possible circumstances, the obligation of convertibility might really prove to be a safeguard against inflation brought about by political pressure contrary to the judgement of the Federal Reserve Board ;—for we have not, as yet, sufficient experience as to the independence of the Federal Reserve system against the farmers, for example, or other compact interests possessing political influence.

Meanwhile Mr. Hoover and many banking authorities in England and America, who look to the dispersion through the world of a reasonable proportion of Washington's gold, by the natural operation of trade and investment, as a desirable and probable development, much misunderstand the situation. At present the United States is open to accept gold at a price in terms of goods above its natural value (above the value it would have, that is to say, if it were allowed to affect credit and, through credit, prices in orthodox pre-war fashion) ; and so long as this is the case, gold must continue to flow there. The stream can be stopped (so long as a change in the gold-value of the dollar is ruled out of the question) only in one of two ways ;—either by a fall in the value of the dollar or by an increase in the value of gold in the outside world. The former of these alternatives, namely the depreciation of the dollar through inflation in the United States, is that on which many English authorities have based their hopes. But it could only come about by a reversal or defeat of the present policy of the Federal Reserve Board. Moreover, the volume of redundant gold is now so great, and the capacity of the rest of the world for its absorption so much reduced, that the inflation would need to be prolonged and determined to produce the required result. Dollar prices would have to rise very high before America's impoverished customers, starving for real goods and having no use for barren metal, would relieve her of £200,000,000 worth of gold in preference to taking commodities. The banking authorities of the United States would be

likely to notice in good time that, if the gold is not
wanted and must be got rid of, it would be much
simpler just to reduce the dollar price of gold. The
only way of selling redundant stocks of anything,
whether gold or copper or wheat, is to abate the
price.

The alternative method, namely the increase in
the value of gold in the outside world, could scarcely
be brought about unless some other country or
countries stepped in to relieve the United States of
the duty of burying unwanted gold. Great Britain,
France, Italy, Holland, Sweden, Argentine, Japan,
and many other countries have fully as much un-
occupied gold as they require for an emergency store.
Nor is there anything to prevent them from buying
gold now if they prefer gold to other things.

The notion, that America can get rid of her gold
by showing a greater readiness to make loans to
foreign countries, is incomplete. This result will only
follow if the loans are inflationary loans, not provided
for by the reduction of expenditure and investment
in other directions. Foreign investments formed out
of real savings will no more denude the United States
of her gold than they denude Great Britain of hers.
But if the United States places a large amount of
dollar purchasing power in the hands of foreigners,
as a pure addition to the purchasing power previously
in the hands of her own nationals, then no doubt
prices will rise and we shall be back on the method

of depreciating the dollar, just discussed, by a normal inflationary process. Thus the invitation to the United States to deal with the problem of her gold by increasing her foreign investments will not be effective unless it is intended as an invitation to inflate.

I argue, therefore, that the same policy which is wise for Great Britain is wise for the United States, namely to aim at the stability of the commodity-value of the dollar rather than at stability of the gold-value of the dollar, and to effect the former if necessary by varying the gold-value of the dollar.

If Great Britain and the United States were both embarked on this policy and if both were successful, our secondary desideratum, namely the stability of the dollar - exchange standard, would follow as a consequence. I agree with Mr. Hawtrey that the ideal state of affairs is an intimate co-operation between the Federal Reserve Board and the Bank of England, as a result of which stability of prices and of exchange would be achieved at the same time. But I suggest that it is wiser and more practical that this should be allowed to develop out of experience and mutual advantage, without either side binding itself to the other. If the Bank of England aims primarily at the stability of sterling, and the Federal Reserve Board at the stability of dollars, each authority letting the other into its confidence so far as may be, better results will be obtained than if sterling is unalterably fixed by law in terms of dollars and the Bank of England is limited to using its influence on the Federal Reserve Board to keep dollars steady. A collaboration which is not free on both sides is likely to lead to dissensions, especially if the business of keeping dollars steady involves a heavy expenditure in burying unwanted gold.

We have reached a stage in the evolution of money when a " managed " currency is inevitable, but we have not yet reached the point when the management can be entrusted to a single authority. The best we can do, therefore, is to have *two* managed currencies, sterling and dollars, with as close a collaboration as possible between the aims and methods of the managements.

III. *Other Countries.*

What course, in such an event, should other countries pursue ? It is necessary to presume to begin with that we are dealing with countries which have not lost control of their currencies. But a stage can and should be reached before long at which nearly all countries have regained the control. In Russia, Poland, and Germany it is only necessary that the Governments should develop some other source of revenue than the inflationary or turn-over tax on the use of money discussed in Chapter II. In France and Italy it is only necessary that the

franc and the lira should be devaluated at a level at
which the service of the internal debt is within the
capacity of the taxpayer.

Control having been regained, there are probably
no countries, other than Great Britain and the United
States, which would be justified in attempting to set
up an independent standard. Their wisest course
would be to base their currencies either on sterling
or on dollars by means of an exchange standard,
fixing their exchanges in terms of one or the other
(though preserving, perhaps, a discretion to vary in
the event of a serious divergence between sterling and
dollars), and maintaining stability by holding reserves
of gold at home and balances in London and New
York to meet short-period fluctuations, and by using
bank-rate and other methods to regulate the volume
of purchasing power, and thus to maintain stability
of relative price level, over longer periods.

Perhaps the British Empire (apart from Canada)
and the countries of Europe would adopt the sterling
standard ; whilst Canada and the other countries of
North and South America would adopt the dollar
standard. But each could choose freely, until, with
the progress of knowledge and understanding, so
perfect a harmony had been established between the
two that the choice was a matter of indifference.

INDEX

GREAT BOOKS IN PHILOSOPHY PAPERBACK SERIES

ESTHETICS

❑ Aristotle—*The Poetics*
❑ Aristotle—*Treatise on Rhetoric*

ETHICS

❑ Aristotle—*The Nicomachean Ethics*
❑ Marcus Aurelius—*Meditations*
❑ Jeremy Bentham—*The Principles of Morals and Legislation*
❑ John Dewey—*The Moral Writings of John Dewey, Revised Edition*
  (edited by James Gouinlock)
❑ Epictetus—*Enchiridion*
❑ Immanuel Kant—*Fundamental Principles of the Metaphysic of Morals*
❑ John Stuart Mill—*Utilitarianism*
❑ George Edward Moore—*Principia Ethica*
❑ Friedrich Nietzsche—*Beyond Good and Evil*
❑ Plato—*Protagoras, Philebus,* and *Gorgias*
❑ Bertrand Russell—*Bertrand Russell On Ethics, Sex, and Marriage*
  (edited by Al Seckel)
❑ Arthur Schopenhauer—*The Wisdom of Life* and *Counsels and Maxims*
❑ Benedict de Spinoza—*Ethics* and *The Improvement of the Understanding*

METAPHYSICS/EPISTEMOLOGY

❑ Aristotle—*De Anima*
❑ Aristotle—*The Metaphysics*
❑ Francis Bacon—*Essays*
❑ George Berkeley—*Three Dialogues Between Hylas and Philonous*
❑ W. K. Clifford—*The Ethics of Belief and Other Essays*
  (introduction by Timothy J. Madigan)
❑ René Descartes—*Discourse on Method* and *The Meditations*
❑ John Dewey—*How We Think*
❑ John Dewey—*The Influence of Darwin on Philosophy and Other Essays*
❑ Epicurus—*The Essential Epicurus: Letters, Principal Doctrines, Vatican Sayings, and Fragments* (translated, and with an introduction, by Eugene O'Connor)
❑ Sidney Hook—*The Quest for Being*
❑ David Hume—*An Enquiry Concerning Human Understanding*
❑ David Hume—*Treatise of Human Nature*
❑ William James—*The Meaning of Truth*
❑ William James—*Pragmatism*
❑ Immanuel Kant—*Critique of Practical Reason*
❑ Immanuel Kant—*Critique of Pure Reason*
❑ Gottfried Wilhelm Leibniz—*Discourse on Metaphysics* and the *Monadology*
❑ John Locke—*An Essay Concerning Human Understanding*
❑ Charles S. Peirce—*The Essential Writings*
  (edited by Edward C. Moore, preface by Richard Robin)
❑ Plato—*The Euthyphro, Apology, Crito,* and *Phaedo*
❑ Plato—*Lysis, Phaedrus,* and *Symposium*
❑ Bertrand Russell—*The Problems of Philosophy*
❑ George Santayana—*The Life of Reason*
❑ Sextus Empiricus—*Outlines of Pyrrhonism*

PHILOSOPHY OF RELIGION

❑ Marcus Tullius Cicero—*The Nature of the Gods* and *On Divination*
❑ Ludwig Feuerbach—*The Essence of Christianity*
❑ David Hume—*Dialogues Concerning Natural Religion*
❑ John Locke—*A Letter Concerning Toleration*
❑ Lucretius—*On the Nature of Things*
❑ John Stuart Mill—*Three Essays on Religion*
❑ Thomas Paine—*The Age of Reason*
❑ Bertrand Russell—*Bertrand Russell On God and Religion* (edited by Al Seckel)

SOCIAL AND POLITICAL PHILOSOPHY

❑ Aristotle—*The Politics*
❑ Mikhail Bakunin—*The Basic Bakunin: Writings, 1869–1871*
   (translated and edited by Robert M. Cutler)
❑ Edmund Burke—*Reflections on the Revolution in France*
❑ John Dewey—*Freedom and Culture*
❑ John Dewey—*Individualism Old and New*
❑ John Dewey—*Liberalism and Social Action*
❑ G. W. F. Hegel—*The Philosophy of History*
❑ G. W. F. Hegel—*Philosophy of Right*
❑ Thomas Hobbes—*The Leviathan*
❑ Sidney Hook—*Paradoxes of Freedom*
❑ Sidney Hook—*Reason, Social Myths, and Democracy*
❑ John Locke—*Second Treatise on Civil Government*
❑ Niccolo Machiavelli—*The Prince*
❑ Karl Marx (with Friedrich Engels)—*The German Ideology*, including
   Theses on Feuerbach and *Introduction to the Critique of Political Economy*
❑ Karl Marx—*The Poverty of Philosophy*
❑ Karl Marx/Friedrich Engels—*The Economic and Philosophic Manuscripts of 1844*
   and *The Communist Manifesto*
❑ John Stuart Mill—*Considerations on Representative Government*
❑ John Stuart Mill—*On Liberty*
❑ John Stuart Mill—*On Socialism*
❑ John Stuart Mill—*The Subjection of Women*
❑ Friedrich Nietzsche—*Thus Spake Zarathustra*
❑ Thomas Paine—*Common Sense*
❑ Thomas Paine—*Rights of Man*
❑ Plato—*The Republic*
❑ Jean-Jacques Rousseau—*The Social Contract*
❑ Mary Wollstonecraft—*A Vindication of the Rights of Men*
❑ Mary Wollstonecraft—*A Vindication of the Rights of Women*

GREAT MINDS PAPERBACK SERIES

CRITICAL ESSAYS

❑ Desiderius Erasmus—*The Praise of Folly*
❑ Jonathan Swift—*A Modest Proposal and Other Satires*
   (with an introduction by George R. Levine)
❑ H. G. Wells—*The Conquest of Time* (with an introduction by Martin Gardner)

ECONOMICS

- Charlotte Perkins Gilman—*Women and Economics: A Study of the Economic Relation between Women and Men*
- John Maynard Keynes—*The General Theory of Employment, Interest, and Money*
- John Maynard Keynes—*A Tract on Monetary Reform*
- Thomas R. Malthus—*An Essay on the Principle of Population*
- Alfred Marshall—*Principles of Economics*
- Karl Marx—*Theories of Surplus Value*
- David Ricardo—*Principles of Political Economy and Taxation*
- Adam Smith—*Wealth of Nations*
- Thorstein Veblen—*Theory of the Leisure Class*

HISTORY

- Edward Gibbon—*On Christianity*
- Alexander Hamilton, John Jay, and James Madison—*The Federalist*
- Herodotus—*The History*
- Thucydides—*History of the Peloponnesian War*
- Andrew D. White—*A History of the Warfare of Science with Theology in Christendom*

PSYCHOLOGY

- Sigmund Freud—*Totem and Taboo*

RELIGION

- Thomas Henry Huxley—*Agnosticism and Christianity and Other Essays*
- Ernest Renan—*The Life of Jesus*
- Elizabeth Cady Stanton—*The Woman's Bible*
- Voltaire—*A Treatise on Toleration and Other Essays*

SCIENCE

- Nicolaus Copernicus—*On the Revolutions of Heavenly Spheres*
- Charles Darwin—*The Descent of Man*
- Charles Darwin—*The Origin of Species*
- Charles Darwin—*The Voyage of the Beagle*
- Albert Einstein—*Relativity*
- Michael Faraday—*The Forces of Matter*
- Galileo Galilei—*Dialogues Concerning Two New Sciences*
- Ernst Haeckel—*The Riddle of the Universe*
- William Harvey—*On the Motion of the Heart and Blood in Animals*
- Werner Heisenberg—*Physics and Philosophy: The Revolution in Modern Science* (introduction by F. S. C. Northrop)
- Julian Huxley—*Evolutionary Humanism*
- Edward Jenner—*Vaccination against Smallpox*
- Johannes Kepler—*Epitome of Copernican Astronomy* and *Harmonies of the World*
- Isaac Newton—*The Principia*
- Louis Pasteur and Joseph Lister—*Germ Theory and Its Application to Medicine* and *On the Antiseptic Principle of the Practice of Surgery*
- Alfred Russel Wallace—*Island Life*

SOCIOLOGY

- Emile Durkheim—*Ethics and the Sociology of Morals* (translated with an introduction by Robert T. Hall)